WEST COUNTRY WICCA

WEST COUNTRY WICCA
A Journal of the Old Religion

by

Rhiannon Ryall

with illustrations by
Diana Green

PHOENIX PUBLISHING INC.

Publisher's Note

Upon reading the manuscript for this book, we immediately felt its potential as a valuable and enjoyable contribution to contemporary Wicca. Although its historical authenticity is difficult to verify, we nonetheless felt that the truths conveyed here are important and meaningful. The portrayal of Wicca in the olden days is at once charming and deeply religious, combining joy, simplicity and reverence. Wisdom shines forth from these pages, the wisdom emanating from country folk who live close to Nature, and a wisdom which can add depth and color to our present understanding of the Craft.

PHOENIX PUBLISHING INC.
P.O. Box 10
Custer, Washington USA 98240

ISBN 0-919345-98-0

Cover design by Rick Testa

Printed in the U.S.A.

Contents

INTRODUCTION

How fortunate we are to have *West Country Wicca!* If only this book had existed when I began my search for traditional witchcraft many years ago my work would have been immeasurably easier. Even today, amidst the popularization of revivalist Wicca and the unprecedented growth of the neo-pagan movement, Rhiannon Ryall is quite a phenomenon: a lifetime member of an ancient pagan community — a hereditary witch.

Hereditary. I wonder if I am speaking just for myself, or for many of us, when I admit to a shiver of something akin to envy whenever I hear of some other witches' claim to that comforting word. I have been a practising witch for many years. But not since birth; not in this lifetime. How many others have felt the same way? Seeking, we have built our own versions of the community Rhiannon describes. Studying, we have reconstructed our own modern versions of the traditions she inherited.

I do not want to diminish the value and power of bringing one's most heartfelt theological ideas into form. So many modern witches have accomplished this unique and brave task. Yet in our quest, in our reinventing, in trying so hard to be accurate, to capture the true meaning of our religion, we may sometimes overlook one key aspect of the Old Religion: *simplicity.* After all, how can one expect to return to some early, natural, unsophisticated state if one has never experienced it in the first place?

Without placing more value on her way than ours, Rhiannon provides for all of us a direct path back to the Old Religion in the British Isles. Her writing is like the conversation of an old family friend, her voice as warm and familiar as that of a dear relative. *This is how it was*, she tells us. *This is the way I remember it.* Both the content of what she remembers, and the form in which she tells us, are straightforward, homespun, and thoroughly unaffected.

This is our Religion.

This is our nature religion.

This is our inheritance, too.

Thank you, Rhiannon Ryall, for sharing your path with us. So this is how it was. Knowing this, we can relax a little.

Marion Weinstein
August, 1989

A thing is complete
when you can
let it
be

—Gita Bellin

THE OLD COUNTRY RELIGION

Another book revealing Rites and Ceremonies of the Old Religion? The prospective reader may well ask this question when such a wide variety of books on this subject already exists. However, the reason for writing this book is because no one from the pre-Gardnerian days has written an account of the Old Religion of that time. I do not have a "title" for my system of craft, except that I was taught in the 1940's, before Gerald Gardner or Alex Sanders had written their books. Indeed, I was unaware of the existence of their writings for many years. We were taught by word of mouth; no notes, nothing at all written down, because most people in those days were illiterate. We had no "Book of Shadows"; in fact we had not heard the phrase at that time. We were told never to discuss the craft with outsiders and had to vow not to.

But now my teachers are all dead, and those who were my contemporaries have moved on, as indeed I have (in my case, to the other side of the world – Australia). I feel now that what I was taught may be of interest to those involved with present day Wicca, perhaps simply as a curiosity from long ago, or perhaps with the thought of adopting some of the rituals of that time. I was not taught by my family as they were not actively involved in the Craft, although most of them were psychic to some degree and two of my aunts were healers. They were, however, aware of the beliefs of the country people. We lived on the Devon/Somerset border and although the system in general may be peculiar to that area, study in later years has led me to believe that some of their customs were quite widespread. The winter rituals in particular have some practices which have popped up in various parts of England.

Teaching the Craft was a very gradual business. Children were encouraged to collect herbs and learn their more arcane uses as well as practical ones. Awareness of the seasons, and the underlying rhythms of the earth, came quite naturally to country children. We were all aware that such customs as the Maypole Dancing and the May Queen had a deeper significance that would be revealed to us when we were older. It was rather like playing with dolls; we realised that it was only a childish copying of adult behaviour that was beyond our understanding as children.

At sixteen, the serious study began. Young men and young women alike were taught by the old women. These women, who were like the Elders of the village, were all well past childbearing age, being at least in their sixties. These were the people that everyone went to for advice and, although very active in the Craft and respected for their wisdom, they did not take the leading role in the ceremony of "Drawing Down The Moon", as only fertile women were considered suitable for this. After initiation, the girls were still taught by the women, but the young men were taught by the old men. This was because only a woman could explain the women's mysteries, and only a man the men's. No man could really explain, for instance, what happened at a "Drawing Down" as he couldn't possibly know what it felt like from a woman's point of view.

The year was divided roughly into two halves. The Goddess ruled from March 25th until October 31st, and the God for the other half of the year. Only five festivals were celebrated. Nothing was known of the two Equinoxes, and Lammas or Imbolg were not celebrated. Although most of the people in the West Country are generally of Celtic descent, they are also very practical. I assume that is why at least two festivals went unnoticed; February and late July/early August are extremely busy times in the country. I understand the Equinoxes are generally held to be of Greek origin. West Country people of that time knew nothing of Mediterranean customs, and therefore did not celebrate either Equinox. Similarly, they had no knowledge of the Descent of the Goddess. As far as they were concerned She rested in the dark months and the God ruled that part of the year.

The five festivals they did celebrate were as follows:

25th March	Lady Day
30th April	Beltane
21st June	Summer Solstice
31st October	Samhain
21st December	Winter Solstice

Beltane always merged into May Day, and it really covered the two days. The ceremonies "ran on", as it were.

Although country people are generally very early to bed, they always seemed to find the stamina to stay up late when necessary. When we met for the Full Moon, for example, it was never until about 11:30pm, and the Circle was up and working at midnight. At a Full Moon ceremony, a large, shallow dish was placed in the Circle to reflect the moon, as it was considered a link for the Drawing Down. No Drawing Down was performed during the winter months. We seemed to have no history or ancestry of Druidism as the Gardnerian/Alexandrian systems so obviously have. (I see nothing wrong with either working but merely point out the differences.) Generally robes were worn, except during the actual Drawing Down and, of course, for initiation.

The robes were mainly brown or black, although for festivals they were usually green. We had no swords and no incense. Wands, made of hazel, willow, or rowan were used. Dried, scented herbs were burnt instead of incense, and sometimes bellows represented the Air element.

The covens were all "closed". In other words, only the Elders of the covens knew the identity of others.

The "witch family tree", which is prevalent nowadays, was unknown. The "family tree" concept indicates that the initiator

and the person being initiated are held together by a bind of psychic bonding. I think that this view has come about with the present day concept of labels, i.e. "Gardnerian", "Alexandrian", etc., where the implication is that somewhere back along the line are those who were initiated by someone who had been, in their turn, initiated by Gardner or Sanders. In my time, the loyalty demanded was to the Old Religion and the Wiccan Path as a whole.

We had only two degrees of initiation, and these were more of a "going in deeper", rather than a climbing of a hierarchal ladder. The Second Degree always consisted, in the main part, of a Great Rite Ceremony. This was accomplished by the leader of another Coven, quite unknown to the Initiate. It was the same for both sexes. One must remember that the Craft was a rural-based religion and that country people were far more matter-of-fact about life, death and procreation than their city counterparts. In fact, I am always amazed how city dwellers try to follow the Old Religion. Living in apartments and working in air-conditioned offices they have, by necessity, brought in ceremonial magic concepts and try to work indoors in "Temples".

In our time the concept of a Temple was unknown. As I have said, the Craft is a religion of the earth, and its practitioners were earthy. They spent their lives surrounded by conception, birth and death in all its many forms, and were therefore more practical and philosophical about these concepts.

I know one very old lady who originates from Central Europe, and was initiated in 1922 by a person born in 1850. Together we have discussed, among other things, the Great Rite, and the fact that many present day people are disturbed by the idea of a possible unwanted conception. The old lady's answer to this was that, if the power is used correctly, that is not taken in and held, it cannot manifest in the physical as a pregnancy because the lifeforce has been used psychically in another way. I cannot better the reply; it says it all.

It is only since my involvement with present day Wicca that I have come across such concepts as the Man in Black, the Charge, the Witches' Rune and, of course, the legend of the Descent of the Goddess.

However, as a male witch of my acquaintance has said, "Just because something is old, it does not necessarily make it more valuable, and just because something is new, it does not mean it has no validity." These sentiments I sincerely endorse. The Witches' Rune, for example, is a very lovely and exciting piece of poetry. The late Gerald Gardner and Doreen Valiente are to be congratulated on the power and beauty of their writings. I have in fact used them in my circle on occasion.

The Charge as well is a very beautiful piece of work, a fine blending of old and new, and much loved by present day witches.

The idea of the Goddess sleeping for some months, and then awakening in the spring, is a foreign concept to most present day Craft people. But the winters in British rural areas are harsh and masculine. The hunting of foxes does not commence until bad weather and game bird shooting begins as summer is ending (August 12th); winter is indeed a time of hunting and death. One must remember that in olden times people could not feed all of their stock during the bitter winters and, in some years, were forced to slaughter all but the breeding stock. Rather than just wantonly take life, this was viewed instead as a religious sacrifice, and who but the God would accept such an offering? Certainly not the gentle Great Mother of the Spring. In our part of the world the God was antlered, and his affectionate name of "Old Horny" is probably from whence the modern day slang derives, meaning sexuality in men.

The Goddess was often called the Green Lady, an acknowledgement of her bountiful love that made the earth bloom. In Devonshire, the God is still looked on as leader of the Wild Hunt. In winter, when gales howl round the chimneys on stormy nights, I have heard locals say, "Wild Hunt's abroad tonight." This comment is always made in the snug warmth of a farmhouse kitchen. I was once asked by a primary school teacher how old country people could have a belief in what she thought of as "Folklore" when they were surrounded by modern technology, even in their homes. I replied that to the old countryman, a television set was a grown up toy, having nothing to do with the "real" world, which is concerned with planting and growing, each in its proper time and place. In this way, the balance in all of life is maintained.

I remember once I was planting some runner beans. An old man from the village, strolling past my garden, saw me and asked me what I was doing. To this day, I can remember the panic I felt, kneeling there, gazing up at him. "Runner beans," I replied, "why, am I too late?" He answered, "No, you'm alright for four days yet." I could have hugged him! If I had planted them out of time, the villagers would have believed that I would upset all the crops in the area. I was thirty-nine at the time but I felt about six years old, and caught transgressing some unknown adult law! They take their care of the earth and its rhythms very seriously, and who is to say they are wrong?

Country people see their God and Goddess everywhere they look: newly hatched chicks, young rabbits on the moors, the sticky buds of the chestnut tree, the acorns from the oaks, and also in the pigs that lust after acorns, like old drunks waiting for opening time at the pub. The God and Goddess are also found in the mistletoe, of course.

In a slow moving rural community, there is always a reluctance to change, a clinging to the old ways. "It was good enough for my father, and his father before him, therefore, it is good enough for me and my children." This tendency does mean, of course, that their rituals, with minor variations, are unchanging. They feel that power has been built up over the years by repetition. This is no doubt so. It is what I call a "well worn path". But I am of the opinion that intent and purpose, coupled with the rhythm, are the power, rather than the words spoken or chanted.

The Roman Catholic Mass is a well worn path, but it has lost so much since forsaking the usage of Latin. As with ceremonial magic, it is the music of the sound that sets up the spiritual vibrations. If this were not so, nothing would have happened in the early days of Alexandrian Craft, and while I was not involved with any Alexandrian coven at any time, and indeed, was unaware of their existence, they must have produced results or they would have foundered. However, while open to change and different systems, I still enjoy using the old rituals I was taught as a young girl.

Newcomers to West Country villages find themselves drawn inexorably into the established pattern. I can remember, in the late sixties, three houses that were being re-thatched. One of them belonged to a young couple that had moved down from a Northern City, to enable them to bring their children up in a healthier, quieter environment. The thatcher on receiving his instructions, said, "You'll be wanting the corn dollies on the roof ends?" This was really more by way of being a statement than a query. The young couple, who were thinking of the cost of their roof, and assuming the dollies would be an extra, replied that, "no thank you, they would forego the decoration." The thatcher, however, could not imagine anyone not wanting the symbols that would ensure all went well, and without which disaster would probably strike the couple, and convinced he had misheard them, provided the dollies anyway.

The corn dollies are of course, a representation of the God and Goddess. They stand at each end of the roof ridge, and guard all within. Similarly, new implements, pitchforks, bellows for the fire, and so forth, have to be "charmed" before they will satisfactorily do the job that they were purchased for.

The old ways permeate all levels of lifestyle. The local veterinarian, who was a young man, would not attend cattle with ringworm as he considered it a waste of money. Anyone new to the area who had taken up farming and experienced this problem in stock was given the name and address of an old man who "charmed" the ringworm away.

The old chap would come out to the farm, the cattle were driven slowly through a cattle race, and the old man held his hands, palms down, about six inches above their bodies as they walked past him. It invariably worked.

One cannot expect such simple, homely people to know how to draw four different elemental pentagrams, or to drive from an element "spirits from the world of phantasm"; it is all too

scholarly and complex. Also, country people, even in this day and age, rarely put pen to paper, and, when I was young, they were even less "scholarly", as they called it, than nowadays. We were taught many things prior to initiation, including casting a circle. Therefore, by the time we were initiated we had a practical working knowledge of the four elements, the reasons for a circle, and how to set one up.

The early passing on of knowledge was a common practice. One must bear in mind that the elders had known us since we were children. Anyone studying the craft invariably carried it through. I have never, to my knowledge, heard of a dropout. We were taught that a magician's circle was cast to keep the magician safe, and that is why the triangle is outside the circle. However, we were told that nothing can harm a witch in her circle as we are working with the natural forces pertaining to the sphere of this planet, and therefore our circle is cast to contain the power within that circle's boundaries, until it is used or sent.

The other main reason for the circle is to move, in a psychic way, that piece of ground encompassed by the boundaries, into another place. It does indeed pass out of this world, into a sort of "no place", where it touches the realms of the Lord and the Lady. We were taught that only a circle, a sort of round boundary, could form an area in touch with the magical realms.

Our elders had never heard of Tattwa symbols and therefore our knowledge of the elements was obtained in a different way. (I must admit that the Tattwas are a much easier method to use than the way we did it, and I have often used them in recent years.) We would fill a cauldron with water and use it to skry that element, or visit a stream and meditate on its waters. With the stream, we could also learn about the Earth, by focusing on little rocks and pebbles that are always plain to see in a clear brook. The other way to know Earth was to go somewhere wild and remote and experience her directly. On a high windy place, utilising the clouds as well, we also contemplated the element of Air. To study Fire, a special fire had to be lit in a specific way. Two flints had to be struck to ignite the kindling. The burning woods consisted of rowan, elder, willow, hazel and oak (five woods). The oak was put on last, as it is impossible to start a fire with oak, even with a magical piece! We were encouraged, as children, to investigate the elements in a very simple way by using the aforementioned methods, and one of the first pieces of magic taught, when we were still very young, was to disperse a small cloud.

At initiation, the initiate's measure was taken with red thread in the form of a spancel. That is, the whole body was outlined, with one person holding the end of the thread on the top of the head, while a second helper completed the measuring. Hair and nail clippings were also taken. No blood was drawn, as the adage "and it harm none" was considered to include pricking a finger to draw blood, whether it was someone else's or a self-inflicted wound. The measure, hair and nail clippings were kept by the elders until the second and final initiation, when they were burnt by the initiate, after the initiation.

Some salt water was poured on the ground with the wine, as a libation, and a cake was saved and crumbled. The sprinkling of salt water when casting was not considered a libation but simply, along with air and fire, the symbolic bringing in of the elements for balance, before they were called for at the quarters.

No one knelt or bowed in a circle as the God and Goddess were not considered omnipotent. For this reason we had to "raise the power"; we felt that our deities needed it to help us, which made it into a two way relationship. This does not mean, of course, that we did not pay reverence to our God and Goddess, but they were viewed in a homey, earthy way. Also, only a person who had gone through the two degrees could experience a Drawing Down, and this was why the second initiation always consisted of a Great Rite. It was believed a "maiden", as a young woman was called, would go insane if Drawn Down upon. Only a "woman", in all senses of the word, could understand and control the power of the Goddess.

When working at phases of the moon, the waxing moon was used for "wish fulfillment" charms. This phase was best for direct magic with intensity reaching its apex at the full moon.

During the waning moon, magical transference decreased day by day, and would, for instance, banish disease if one's arms up to the elbows were submerged in a flowing stream.

We always cast Circles near oak trees and running water. Covens generally only met at the full moon, although there were exceptions, such as when work against Foot and Mouth disease was necessary.

Only four elemental weapons were used: Cup, knife, wand and a flat dish for salt. The Wand was made of hazel, willow or rowan wood. No Sword, Scourge or Cords were on the altar.

At Beltane and at Handfastings everyone would leap over the fire.

Some areas did "beating the bounds" on Lady Day.

All the girls washed in dew on May Morning.

Any children born as a result of the "Balefire" (Beltane) were known as Merrybegots.

To make anointing oil, lavender, rosemary and rose oils, witch hazel, and castor oil were used. Sometimes crushed acorns or rowan berries were steeped in the oil and then strained off.

Scented lamp oil, or dried crushed herbs, were used for the Air element.

We believed the spirit of the corn would wither or go away when the last sheaf was cut, so the corn dolly was made from the last sheaf, for the spirit to live in until the next harvest. This corn dolly was known as the "maiden".

A small part of the other crops were dug in "to give thanks to the earth". Eggs also were sometimes buried.

We would drink blackberry, elderberry, dandelion wine, or cider.

This then, is a brief introduction to the background in which I grew up, and learned the "Lore of the Wise". I hope that my account of the old religion as it existed in the pre-Gardnerian days will be able to add something of value to the practice of the Craft today and that the simple wisdom from those days will continue to live on in the rituals of the future.

THE RITUALS

TOOLS OF THE CRAFT

The Athame, Wand, Goblet, and Dish were the main tools. Usually two goblets were used, one for the water and one for the wine. A dish was used for the salt, and another for the cakes. We had no swords, scourges or pentacles. The binding cords were of thin rope, and these were kept for that purpose only.

During the final weeks of learning, the Initiate had to make a robe cord, usually green, or green and silver, or green, silver and gold, which generally contained forty knots. When finished, the cord had to measure four and a half feet long so that it could be used to mark out a nine foot circle.

A necklace of acorns was also fashioned, and these had to be threaded on stout thread that had been rubbed thoroughly with beeswax.

The athame was usually made by the blacksmith.

The dish for salt was usually carved of wood, as was the goblet for the water.

The wine goblet was pewter or silver.

The Circle would be nine or eighteen feet wide, depending on how many were to attend. Non-Initiates attended Full Moon ceremonies and saw the Circle cast, but left again before the Drawing Down. If there was no Drawing Down they stayed until the end.

This resulted in two types of ceremonies. The first one that I will describe was used when all present were initiated.

CIRCLE CEREMONY WITH
INITIATES PRESENT

We would light the fire before starting any other activities. Then the circumference of the Circle was swept with a broom made of broom (the shrub of the plantagenat family), circling in the direction of the sun. The Circle was cast with the athame, starting and ending in the North. On the altar was one goblet containing spring or river water; another one containing wine. A flat, wooden platter held rock salt, the dish of cakes, and one candle, which was lit after the sweeping. Once we had cast the Circle, we would bring the altar candle to the quarters, and light the four elemental candles. Our altar was in the north, but slightly inside the Circle, so that the north candle stood behind the altar. If we had no fire, the altar was placed in the centre of the Circle.

It was decided, before the ceremony, who would cast the Circle and call the quarters, i.e. "Set the Wards". The coven leaders were not known as High Priest and High Priestess but, as this is common usage nowadays, I will refer to the coven leaders as High Priest and Priestess in order to avoid confusion.

After the quarter candles were lit, the quarter elements were brought into the Circle as an actual sign that the elements were now involved.

The athame was plunged into the goblet of water with the words, "I cleanse thee, O creature of water and charge thee in the name of the Lord and the Lady." Then the salt was consecrated. The knife tip was put into the salt with these words: "Blessings be upon this creature of salt in the name of the Lord and the Lady." The salt was then tipped into the water and stirred with the knife. Then, going with the sun, round the edge of the Circle, water would be sprinkled with the words, "I purify with water and earth."

After this, a dish of burning dried herbs was carried round, with the words, "I scent this Circle with air." And last the altar candle was carried round with the words, "I warm this Circle with fire."

This completed, either the same person or another would go to the North, raise the athame aloft, and say, "I call upon Earth the power to make," then the East, "I call upon Air the power to take," then the South, "I call upon Fire the power to grow," and then the West, "I call upon Water, the power to flow."

Then everyone circling, with the sun, would chant,

> "Green power and gold, red power and blue,
> Here the power we do unfold,
> Quarters' might, strong and true.
> Four the winds to weave the round,
> 'tween the worlds the power be bound.
> Till we send it at the last,
> Guardians keep it strong and fast."

After the chant one person would return to the altar, and raising up the athame, call upon the Lord and Lady to attend.

As previously mentioned, a shallow water-filled pan was placed in the Circle for a Full Moon Rite, so that the moon's reflection could be seen in the water. With her back to the North, and this dish at her feet, the High Priestess was ready for the Drawing Down. The High Priest faced her, with the dish of water between them, and after feeling he had drawn the God-Force into himself, he would say,

> "O Gracious Goddess, behold thy Priestess...(her name),
> Bring down thy power upon her and within her,
> That through thy Great Art, she may see those things
> Which are hidden, and know thy wisdoms which she lacks.
> O Lady of the Fields, enter now thy Priestess...(her name)."

After the Drawing Down, they exchanged the Fivefold Salute, the High Priest saluting first.

The object of the Drawing Down was threefold: one, to bring Power into the Circle; two, so that the Priestess in question

might receive messages, or flashes of insight that would benefit all; and three, we felt it was really the main religious ceremony of Wicca.

After the Drawing Down we danced to heighten the power and, while everyone kept in mind what the power was to be used for, the following was chanted while dancing,

> "Air wheel, Air blow, turn the wheel of magic so.
> Grind the power we send to you.
> HU! HU! HU! HU!
> Fire bright, fire burn, make the mill of magic turn,
> Work the power we send to you.
> HU! HU! HU! HU!
> Water bubble, water flow, make the wheel of magic go,
> Spin the power we send to you.
> HU! HU! HU! HU!
> Earth ye be our kith and kin, make the mill of magic spin,
> Send the power we send to you.
> HU! HU! HU! HU!"

Then all would stand and concentrate on the purpose that the power was being used for. Sometimes the purpose was chanted aloud, and sometimes the concentration was silent, depending on which was most appropriate.

The work completed, everyone would participate in the ceremony of cakes and ale, or cakes and wine, depending on the drink. To bless the wine a man held the goblet while a woman plunged the knife into it saying,

> "Blessings be upon this fruit of the vine,
> But before the cup was filled the seed was planted,
> And so we remember and bless thee both."

For blessing the cakes, the woman placed the point of her knife onto the cakes, saying,

"Bless this food which comes from the bountiful womb.
May all partake of thy wisdom and strength."

To banish the Circle everyone would circle with the sun, starting in the East, athame held aloft, and say,

"We thank thee for thy goodwill,
And ere ye return to the Isles of the Blest,
We say Hail and Farewell."

This was repeated at all four quarters, then, at the North, all faced this quarter and said,

"O Gracious Goddess and noble God,
We thank thee for blessing this Circle
And ere ye return to the Isles of the Blest,
We say Hail and Farewell."

At the end a libation of water and wine were poured onto the ground, and a cake crumbled.

Wicca is a very democratic path—all are equal in the sight of the Lady. Some simply have more knowledge than others. The Circle belongs to all who are in it. I have heard people in recent times say, "I wouldn't have such and such in MY circle." These comments are made by what is now called a High Priest or High Priestess. But it is not THEIR circle. It is the circle of the coven. We had no permanent leaders when I was taught. One person would cast the Circle. One or two more, or perhaps even four, would call the quarters. Two others blessed the wine and cakes. Everyone participated equally.

Adventurous children played in the Circle. Some, of course, were nervous about entering, but many did. It was a place of love for all, and belonged to all. In fact sometimes when we met we would find daisy chains or pretty stones on the altar, or at the quarters, that had been placed there by the children during the day.

As I have stated previously, non-initiates were allowed in a Circle, so that they would be able to get a feel for the ceremonies. It is to this day the only sure way I have of assessing whether a person has "got it", or not. Of course, when I was taught, the question did not arise. But nowadays, with so many new converts to Wicca, it is the only way to know whether they are right for the Craft. If, after three participations, a newcomer does not experience what the rest of us feel within a Circle, I turn them away. Many people get caught up in the form and mystery, and think the magic is "out there" somewhere. If they do no feel it WITHIN, they are not right for the Craft.

CIRCLE CEREMONY WITH NON-INITIATES PRESENT

The Circle would be cast in the usual way, including sweeping with the broom twig bundle.

To address the Quarters, one person started in the middle near the fire, and moving swiftly round the Circle, going with the sun, athame held aloft, called out:

> "Ho! East, South, West, North!
> Here I come to call ye forth.
> Attend ye here with joy and mirth,
> Air and Fire, Water and Earth."

The remainder of the Circle casting was as usual. The salt and water were consecrated in the usual way and taken round, as was the air and fire.

We would not perform any work, unless one of the non-initiates had a request. We would also omit Drawing Down the Moon. Instead, after the Circle was cast, the trainees were encouraged to sit around the fire and meditate. We would also circle dance to raise power, but without any chanting. We wanted to find out if the new people were feeling anything and, if so, what.

After this the cakes and wine were blessed in a somewhat different way. The Priest held the goblet in his left hand, with the Priestess placing her knife across the goblet to make a little shelf. On the knife blade was placed a cake. The Priestess put one hand over this, while the Priest placed his right hand over hers, whereupon she said,

"Bless this wine we share with thee,
And the little moony cake.
Strengthen bonds twixt thee and me,
As of this we do partake."

Cakes and wine were then shared in the usual manner.

When banishing the Circle, we circled rapidly, going with the sun, while the following was chanted,

"North, East, South, West.
Now begone and take thy rest.
From the Lady be thou blest,
North, East, South, West."

And then we made the final offering of water, wine and cake.

It was quite usual to have a "Tine" set up to represent the God and Goddess. Generally they were put up for both. These were pitchforks, set upright in the ground, one on each side of the altar. At Festivals they would be decorated. Some covens had the two pronged fork for the God, and the three pronged for the Goddess, while others reversed them. It didn't really matter however, and no one objected to someone having a preference different from their own.

When anointing before working, the anointing oil was put on the middle of the brow, just above the bridge of the nose. It was marked in a crescent moon shape. Some people also traced the points relating to the Fivefold Salute. Non-Initiates simply had a spot of oil on their foreheads.

The rituals were, as is obvious, very simple.

If the weather was bad, the ceremonies were held in a barn. In this case a hay barn with open sides was used, usually for November Eve or Yule. (There must have been some May Eves when the weather was bad, but I cannot recall one.) Candle lanterns then replaced fires, and the fire in the middle burned in a fire pot.

Should the high priestess happen to find that the ceremony of Drawing Down the Moon at Full Moon coincided with an awkward "time of the month", she still took the main role, and merely kept her robe on. A woman's "time of the month" was considered magically very significant. It was preferred, in fact, to have a menstruating woman take the lead part in a Drawing Down, as it was felt she was imbued with extra power at this time. It emphasized her female nature. That is why a woman past the age of child bearing did not take the priestess role in the Drawing Down.

The pan of water in the circle to catch the Moon was usually a china bowl from a washstand jug and bowl set.

The old tradition had no ritual for a couple breaking up, as such did not occur very often in the country. In all the years I lived there, I never heard of a couple splitting up, Craft or otherwise.

The isolation of the farms, and the long hours spent working on the land, left little time for going many miles into a town to seek more sophisticated company and entertainment. Many people never visited outside the district they lived in.

Today the proliferation of cars has brought many visitors, and new faces, to some rural areas, but the old time country dwellers are still very set in their ways.

When I was a child, a woman who wore makeup was unknown. The women even used to knit their stockings from brown wool!

Some years ago, when electricity was being offered to some areas that didn't have it (there are still places that will never have electricity, as the terrain is too difficult), one woman announced she did not want it, as all it meant to her was an extra bill every three months.

One very old lady, who decided to have electricity, thought it was marvellous, as she could see to light her oil lamps, where-upon she turned the electric light off again!

We also had no rite for a person who had "gone on". Grief was a very personal business, and, anyway, the family went through the form of funeral and church burial, which I think they found harrowing enough. Most people, even those of the Craft, observed the form of going to church on Sundays. There were two reasons for this: firstly was that it would be remarked upon if they did not (not all country dwellers are Craft), and most churches in the West were built on Pagan Sites anyway.

RITE OF INITIATION

The Rite of Initiation was generally carried out in a cave. If for some reason this was not possible, it took place among trees in a copse or small wood. The Initiate would be led to this spot, bound and blindfolded, and then left to ponder, while the others lit the Circle fire, cast the Circle, and worked with the elements. When all of this was finished, and if they thought the Initiate had been left long enough, a doorway was made in the Circle, and all filed out and went to the cave. A doorway was opened by simply moving the hands apart, and closed again by bringing the hands together.

When everyone had assembled at the cave mouth, the initiate was called to crawl out. The Coven members stood astride, so that the Initiate had to crawl out through their legs, and the coveners would call out, guiding the Initiate. Not surprisingly, this often turned into quite a jolly affair, with everyone urging the Initiate on. When the Initiate had passed through the first person's legs, that one then moved away, and back towards the Circle. After the Initiate had crawled through the last pair of legs, their owner would lead the Initiate to the Circle edge, where everyone else was waiting.

The Initiate was guided through the Circle doorway which was then re-sealed. At this point their blindfold and bonds were removed. All this was enacted in an atmosphere of great good

humour—there really isn't a great deal of solemnity in the Old Craft!

Now the Initiate had to be rubbed all over with a mixture of warmed oil and wine, which had a twofold purpose: they were being anointed with fire and water (the initiate having already experienced earth and air), and it warmed them up after their ordeal. In a cold climate, this can be a very chilly occasion! I was initiated, in a cave, just after my eighteenth birthday, in November, and I do not recall any other time when I was so frozen as I was that night!

The Initiate, after being marked with oil on the forehead and the back of the heel, picked up their own athame, which had already been placed on the altar earlier, and swore, "I do solemnly swear to harm no one by word or deed. I will be faithful to the Lady and her Lord. I will be faithful and true to my companions on the Hidden Path. I will not reveal the secrets of the Art, except to someone with the Mark of the Goddess on them."

This completed, the Initiate was paraded round the Circle, while the others chanted: "Behold...(Witch Name), she/he treads the Secret Way, and is blessed."

The initiation over, everyone put on their robes, consecrated the cakes and wine and celebrated.

SECOND AND FINAL INITIATION

As I have mentioned earlier, we had only two degrees of initiation. The second initiation was really a sign that the witch had sufficient knowledge and maturity of mind to do any kind of magical work necessary, should he or she ever have to work on their own.

This final rite never took place until at least a year and a day had passed since the first initiation. In the meantime, the women taught the women, and the men taught the men.

Among other things, women learned of the significance of the "Cauldron of Cerridwen", or the cauldron of knowledge, and the symbolism it and the wine blessing contained. They were also taught what to expect at a Drawing Down the Moon rite, and the altered state of consciousness that occurs. In those days it was not called an "altered state", of course, as they were quite unfamiliar with such expresssions; they called it "being filled with the Goddess" (in a man, the God). Of course, a lot of practical experience was accumulated too, in subjects such as herbal lore, healing, the significance of some animals, and divination. Both sexes were taught all of this. In addition, the men had their own rituals as well. Everyone joined in the Winter Festivals but from November Eve until Lady Day the men worked alone. As stated before, no Drawing Down was done during these months.

Women spent the winter months teaching, making oils, drying herbs, brewing wine and making robes.

In times of great hardship, such as during an outbreak of that dreadful cattle disease, Foot and Mouth, everyone would turn out and work. We always had theories as to why this disease had occurred. It only affects animals that have split or cloven hooves, leading to the thought that the Goddess protected animals sacred to her, such as horses. Therefore, as the disease did not result because of an omission on HER behalf, this only left the God.

As a result of his reasoning, work that was executed for this disease involved a Drawing Down of the God force into a male witch. We would burn purifying herbs which were then used by farmers whose stock was not afflicted as well as those who had sick beasts. These herbs were mixed with tar, and painted on the animals' hooves.

To describe the final initiation I will first depict the ceremony for a woman's initiation.

We dipped water from a stream and stirred it with an oaken wand, before consecrating it. Apple rings and apple blossoms (dried if not in the spring) decorated the altar, in addition to holly and ivy leaves twined together. Basil, bayleaf, celandine and cinnamon were burned and also strewn in the Circle. The

dish contained quartered apples instead of Sabbat cakes. The annointing oil consisted of the oil of roses.

The circle would be swept with the bundle of broom, drawn with a wand, and cast with a knife.

Then the Initiate's measure would be placed on the altar, along with her hair and nail clippings.

After the quarters were completed, we danced to raise power; everyone dancing with their back to the Circle.

Robed and blindfolded, the Initiate stood near the centre, and then was led to each quarter and introduced. Tines for the God and Goddess were on each side of the altar, where the Initiate and the High Priest stood. The Initiate reaffirmed her first oaths, and expressed readiness for her next step, with knowledge of the fact that power would be bestowed.

The altar was cleared, all that was on top being put at the sides by the Tines. For this initiation, the altar would consist of a great piece of wood, resting on two big logs. The High Priest, from another coven, was unknown to the Initiate. He wore a mask of rigid material covering the top half of his face and across his nose. The mask was covered with rabbit skin, and had antlers fastened to it. Robe and blindfold were removed from the Initiate, who was then lifted onto the altar.

A doorway was cut in the Circle, and all except the High Priest and Initiate filed out, closing the doorway behind them.

The Great Rite now took place, and the Initiate had to throw power at the crucial moment so that those outside the Circle could sense or feel it.

Then the Initiate was helped down from the altar by the High Priest, whereupon they performed the ritual of Drawing Down the Moon.

After the Drawing Down, the High Priest blew a horn made of a cow's horn three times, signaling the others to come back to the Circle. Re-opening the doorway, they entered, and closed it again behind them.

Everything was placed back on the altar; the High Priest and Initiate consecrated the apples and wine, and then spoke together:

"Here where sword and cup unite,
Witnessed by the secret night,
Within the charmed Circle's bound,
Behold the Hallows meaning found.
I am in thee, and thee in me,
That is the deepest Mystery."

Others responded:

"Though other bonds of kith and kin,
Diminish, weaken, or grow dim,
This shining cord that binds us all,
Will last and hold 'till earth shall fall."

And the High Priest and Inititate replied,

"Rent the veil,
The magic trod,
Bathed by the light
That grows not dim,
Greeted by our
Joan the Wad,
Beyond the edge
Of this world's rim."

The rest said,

"We who are Guardians of the Way,
Bound as one by word and deed,
No weal of wight can us gainsay,
As we follow our true rede,
To work and make and love and bless,
'till Old Ones call us to Lyonesse."

Again the Priest and Initiate spoke,

"Cloaked in truth no weal or wight
Can harm us by charm or deed,
To work and make and love and bless,
And meet once more in Lyonesse."

Following these words the Initiate then banished the Circle.

It will be understood that there was not much celebration after this initiation as it was a great ordeal, tiring, and very, very magical. For most Initiates the Drawing Down was quite overwhelming on this first occasion. At this particular time a tremendous power existed within the Circle.

When a man was being initiated, everything was exactly the same, except that he lifted himself onto the altar, the anointing oil was cinnamon, and the High Priestess drew the God force into him. Again, the High Priestess was completely unknown to the man, and she wore a mask of silk, on a stiffened back, that covered the top half of her face and was surmounted by a crescent moon. Over this she wore a veil that came over her head completely and covered her shoulders. She removed this veil after the Great Rite.

These, then were the only two initiations required. It was tacitly understood that everyone would eventually experience the final initiation and therefore the covens did not always have the same leaders. Everything was decided on consensus, with the Elders being consulted as the final arbiters, should it be needed.

The rituals were, of course, known to all, and we had no written rituals which are so prevalent today. While this meant no change in the ceremonies, it did preclude the "reading of scripts", which is quite common in contemporary Australia. No one can concentrate and feel what is happening while they are waiting to read what to do next.

Today there is a lack of spontaneity in the Circle. Instinctive joy is giving place to solemn reverence, which is fostered by the hierarchical system. The Craft was never meant to be structured and serious. While my comments may seem contradictory in that knowing the rituals by heart would seem to negate spontaneity, it does, in fact, have the opposite effect. One example is the Charge. There is no way I could recite something during a Drawing Down ceremony. One is simply "not here". To speak brings one "back down", and therefore blocks the very effect the Drawing Down should have.

I defy anyone who is completely involved in the ceremony to be able to speak. Indeed, both Priest and Priestess need a few moments afterwards to "come down to earth" before they bless the cakes and wine. Also, others in the Circle should be involved in the magical change that takes place during this rite. One custom here has coven members file past the Priestess and pay some sort of homage to her after the Drawing Down. I disagree with this completely. The whole group should have benefited from the environment at this time. The Priestess actively involved in the ceremony is merely the key that unlocks the door, and the Goddess Power brought down into the Circle is for the benefit of all. Above everything else, the Craft is a sharing philosophy, with all being equal, and all sharing in whatever manifests in the Circle.

When two people who have a lot of experience in Craft decide to teach newcomers, then of course they know more, but that is all. Decisions about when to bring other people in, or who should do what, are the concern of all in the coven.

There is a tendency among some people to develop a mystique, as opposed to the Mysteries. It takes the form of, "I know something you don't know, and you are not ready yet to know it, or I shall have lost my superiority." I am of the opinion that anyone who knows the right question to ask is ready for the answer.

Maybe I will be criticised for my comments, but the last thing the Craft needs is to become elitist and too structured or we shall end up as hide-bound as the Christian Church.

The Craft is simply a worship, through nature, of the One Supreme Initiator and a caring for everything on this planet. We are not engaging in amateur dramatics, with wardrobes and props; we are joyfully celebrating life in all its many forms.

WICCANNING AND HANDFASTING

A baby was not given a Craft name at Wicanning. He or she was often referred to as the son or daughter of, for example, Joan and Robin. These would be the parents' Craft names. The baby was called by the name that the parents would use everyday.

I know it can be customary now for witches to have up to four names, including one only they know. With so many names to remember, I would be in danger of forgetting the secret name I had myself!

Originally, the purpose of a Craft name was two-fold. Firstly, it accorded secrecy back in the times of the persecution. If one only knew the Craft name of a person, and was vague about their dwelling place, there would be little chance of betraying them to the witchfinder.

The second reason for having a Craft name was, of course, the age-old belief in the power of a person's true name. Letting the coven know of one's true name was another instance of the concept of "perfect love and perfect trust."

The way an initiate received their Craft name had to be inspirational. If an initiate, with the best will in the world, could not "feel" what their name was or should be, the Elders pondered on the matter and provided the initiate with what was considered to be their true name. At other times, the Elders were inspired to give an initiate their Craft name. One of the Elders would say during training that a particular person's name was such and such. This is how I received mine, which is Celtic Welsh even though I am half Irish!

RITE OF WICCANNING

Wiccanning a baby was a very simple affair.

The Circle, cast in the usual way, was nine feet wide, and the altar and quarters were decorated with flowers.

After the calling of the quarters, salt water would be mixed with a small amount of anointing oil and wine. With this mixture we marked a crescent on the baby's forehead, saying "I sign thee...(baby's name)...with the mark of the Goddess. May she ever protect thee and guide thy steps along her pathways."

Next a candle was moved over the child as one of us stated, "May the love of the Goddess ever warm thee."

Burning herbs were gently waved over the child to the words, "May the breath of the Goddess ever bless thy heart."

After this, the God and Goddess were called upon to hear the child's name, and whose child he/she was. The child was then presented at the quarters, after which cakes and wine were consecrated and passed around, with a libation poured onto the earth.

And then we banished the Circle.

If the baby was very small, we usually worked the Rite of Wiccaning during daylight hours.

RITE OF HANDFASTING

For the Rite of Handfasting, the Circle would be eighteen feet wide and decorated with flowers, leaves and flower petals. Horseshoes were placed around the candles at each quarter.

If possible, the Priest and Priestess who had initiated the couple presided over the ceremony.

We conducted the Circle casting as usual.

The couple would be annointed and presented at the quarters by their witch names. Both donned circlets of flowers which had been kept on the altar until their entry. A pathway to the Circle was formed by strewing the ground with leaves and petals; a doorway was cut in the Circle allowing the couple to enter and then re-sealed.

Each vowed to be true to the other, to be helpmates, and to apply their Wiccan tenets to the union. The couple vowed all this as the "Hidden Children of the Goddess." Usually the Priestess asked the man first; after his reply, the Priest asked the woman.

A double sized wreath of flowers, large enough to embrace the two, was placed around their necks by an Elder, usually a woman, who would speak the following:

"May the binding of this handfasting bond be felt as lightly as this garland. It is a bond of love, equally shared, not a chain of servitude. I will tell you the Wiccan Law, which should be reflected in your marriage.

THIS BE THE LAW

That thou lovest all things in nature, for they are the
Gifts of the God and Goddess. That thou bring harm to none
By word or deed. That thou go modestly in this realm
And thy feet stray not from the Hidden Path.
Contentment shalt thou find in simple things and,
At the last, thou will meet again in the Summer Land."

Usually this Wiccan Law was given to the couple as an embroidered sampler. I have seen some beautiful needlework made for young couples.

The double wreath they wore was removed and placed on the altar, whereupon both held hands and leaped the fire. This was followed by the ceremony of cakes and wine. After this ceremony we rang a bell and blew a horn at each quarter and the newly weds were introduced as a truly joined couple. They then poured libations and crumbled cakes, after which came feasting and celebration.

In fine weather, the pair would go off afterwards into the woods to consummate the wedding. (I am not sure if this is the true origin of the saying "Greenwood Wedding" or whether it applies to the "unofficial" pairings of May Eve!)

If, by chance, the ceremony was performed in a barn because of bad weather, everyone would leave the couple alone after the celebration to consummate their wedding within the circle. Afterwards, they banished the Circle themselves.

MALE RITUALS

As I have mentioned, women did not work in the winter months. Men, however, did, but in a way different from the women. November Eve and Yule, it will be noted, are very masculine in content.

If the men worked at the Full Moon, I never heard of it. This does not mean that I can swear on oath that they did not, but, if they did, they must have kept extremely quiet about it. The only time I know that men did work during a Full Moon was on the odd occasion such as sickness in the cattle, as has already been mentioned earlier. At these times the women worked with them as well.

However, our men did have some very masculine rites that were worked in daylight.

In November, the blacksmith made four horseshoes. These were cooled in pig's blood obtained from an animal that was being killed for meat.

Four corners of a field were left unploughed and the horseshoes were buried at the four corners (the corners generally were in correspondence to the quarters). The horseshoes were buried going round with the sun.

After this was done, the remainder of the pig's blood was sprinkled on the furrows.

In January, the blacksmith built a special fire and fed small bits of metal and coal into it. When the fire cooled down, the embers and the bits of clinker were taken and put into a full river, with some blood and some seeds.

In February, a scarecrow was made containing a few bits of fur, feather and a few bones from a gamekeeper's pole. Also, if lambing started early, a piece of afterbirth was buried in the same field with the horseshoes and the scarecrow.

These little rituals were most likely remnants of a time when the Craft was more primitive than it is today.

Another curiosity that was particularly male, called "Crying

the Neck" or "Crying the Knack", was enacted at harvest time, in the last field of barley being cut.

While the last of the barley was being harvested, a man, usually the owner of the field, would go round the stooks, taking one ear of barley from each. These he would fasten into a neat bundle and tie it with one of the ears of barley. Then he would go to the middle of the field, lay his hat down and hold the little sheaf of barley above his head.

All the other men would gather round him in a circle, and also lay their hats down. The man holding the sheaf crouched down so that the bundle touched the ground, and then straightened up and held it aloft again. This action was repeated three times. The others imitated his movements; each time the sheaf was held high the rest of the men would cry out, "The neck, the neck, he has the neck!"

At this point, the man with the "neck" would start to run. If they were in a home field, he would run towards the farmhouse, but if they were near the village he would run towards the blacksmith's. All the other men would chase him, with cries of "the neck!", "the neck!", and they would try to get the neck for themselves. Whoever had it would cry while still running, "I've got 'un! I've got the neck!"

He who had the neck, when he reached either farmhouse or forge, would run to the pump and pump water onto it, after which he would hang it up in his kitchen and keep it until the next harvest.

The "neck" obviously brought good luck, and I think that its wetting was to ensure good rain at the right time. This is most certainly another ritual that has its origins in a darker time of the Craft's history, and is most likely a remnant of the sinister "Barley Dream".

I was told the story of the "Barley Dream" as it has been handed down but, of course, no one could remember a time when this rite was still practiced, and even the oldest people had, in their time, never known anyone who could remember it. Nonetheless, it was a ritual from the far past, and we were told of its details.

In the days when they sacrificed the Corn King, the person who was the King of the Barley or Corn was given a ritual drink before going "into the Corn."

This drink had in it, among other things, hemp and dwale. It was, I should imagine, like taking opium and LSD at the same time.

Therefore, when the King was taken into the barley field, he was in a dreamlike state, and quite unaware of any reality at all. The man was already in a world of his own and out of touch with the real events taking place.

They used to sever the arteries and, in his dreamlike state, the Corn King quietly slipped from life to death. He dreamed his way into the corn.

That, I was told, was the dreadful "Barley Dream."

With the blacksmith having an important role in the Old Religion, and with our knowledge of myths, such as that of Weyland Smith, the blacksmith of the Old English Gods, it seems a fair assumption that what is now the village Smith was, in years gone by, the Shaman of the Tribe or village.

Blacksmiths are still quite significant in the life of a village. They make Craft weapons, generally have a leading role in male rituals, and are considered a vital link with the magical past.

It was a trade that was generally passed on from father to son, or grandfather to grandson.

In a branch of the Craft that is without Druidic influence, it would seem logical that the male role was originally shamanistic, and that the women were involved in what has now come to be the Craft in its entirety.

Obviously, men and women would have worked together, and then each coven would have consisted of a whole small community, with their own village Shaman.

I am, of course, talking about very long ago, probably nearly back to the dawn of civilisation.

Customs in the West Country, however, would have lingered on far longer than in the rest of England. Cornwall, in particular, remained Pagan long after the rest of England had embraced Christianity.

THE FESTIVALS

You will notice that a lot of coming and going in and out of the Circle occured during some Festivals. We felt that the Circle belonged to all; therefore anyone could make and re-seal a doorway. Everyone had the boundaries in their mind's eye, so they could easily visualize the opening and closing.

Also, it was thought that nothing nasty could or would get into a Circle, for the power inside was too strong. In any event, at the level at which Wicca is practiced, we believed there was little likelihood of anything really bad being around.

Everyone in the area knew where the Circles were, and anyone was at liberty to sit in one during the day, whether they were Craft or not. Similarly, no one objected to animals within in its bounds either, as they are all Children of the Goddess in their own way. (I have mentioned previously that children sometimes played in the Circle.)

LADY DAY
Festival of the Return of the Goddess (25th March.)

March 25 is generally accepted in the West Country of England as the day the Goddess returns. When I was a child it was the official day that farms changed hands, regardless of what time of the year the actual sale took place.

Our Circle would be eighteen feet wide, and both it and the altar were decorated with wild flowers. The God and Goddess

35.

tines, too, were wreathed with leaves and flowers. We wore green robes.

After the Circle was cast and the Quarters and wards set in the usual way, the Priestess stood near the fire, in the centre, but on the east side of the fire. She would hold a sheaf of daffodils, enough so that all present could receive one. The Priest stood on the opposite side of the fire in the West.

Everyone else circled with the sun, chanting,

> "Greet we now our Lady,
> Returning with the Spring.
> Bringing back the greening,
> Swift and Swallows Wing."

All then stood still while the Priestess moved round the Circle, handing each a flower, and saying,

> "I am the Great Green Goddess,
> I am the deep red earth.
> I am She Eternal,
> Quickening all to birth.
> I am Sower of seed, Moon Maiden,
> Yet Mother to all that grows,
> Nettle and Gorse and Heather,
> White May in the tall hedgerows."

She then went back to the centre, while all danced round again, chanting,

> "Blessed now the hilltop,
> Blessed now the stream.
> Oak and ash and birchwood
> Wake from winter's dream.
> Wake ye mystic rowan,
> Enchanted hazel, HO!
> Slumber not old willow
> Nor dread mistletoe."

The Priest, wearing antlers, then handed her a flower-decorated wand, and they faced each other.

The Priestess spoke:

> "Returned am I in gladness,
> To conjoin with the One.
> Antlered, bold yet gentle,
> Soft Moon blend with bright Sun."

After the Priest and Priestess exchanged a Fivefold Salute, the Cakes and Wine were consecrated.

They then buried an egg at each Quarter, whereupon all the others would file out.

The Priest and Priestess then celebrated the Great Rite.

Afterwards the Priest would blow a horn to bring everyone else back into the Circle, and a general celebration took place.

The festivals were always a time of light-hearted celebration, and unless it was absolutely vital, no work was performed at these times.

BELTANE
Festival of May Eve (May 1)

One of the two great fire festivals, May Eve was always very Bacchanalian in content. As I have remarked, country people are very earthy and close to nature; May Eve epitomised these rural qualities.

The Circle was eighteen feet, and hay stooks were placed around the outside at the Quarters. Green branches were laid to form a pathway to the Circle. A fire burned in its centre as well as on hilltops all around.

That year's May Queen was not present. She would be crowned the following morning, and had to be what is politely called a "Maiden". It was thought that if she went to the Belfire, she might not be "virgo intacta" next day. So she had to stay at home!

Garlands were set up on the Maypole during daylight hours in readiness for the next day; the garlands the May Queen's attendants would wear were also made at this time. May Eve and May Day are very busy times from a Craft point of view.

The Sabbat cakes were special: round, not crescent shaped and we ate sponge finger type cakes as well. We wore our green robes.

Flowers were abundant, and both Tines were decorated with many blossoms. Sometimes pets were brought in to be blessed by the elements.

We cast the Circle and called the Quarters in the normal way, and immediatedly afterwards the Cakes and Wine ceremony was held, whereupon spiral and back to back dances were performed—all very jolly!

Sometimes we jumped the fire, and if a couple leaped together they were considered betrothed. If a single girl jumped alone, it was believed she would be fertile; not a very desirable attribute at Beltane!

When the fire started to die down, or when everyone thought it time, a doorway was cut in the circle, and all the young ones went off "a-maying." They returned at dawn, bringing fresh greenery for May Day. The girls all bathed their faces with dew. Then, the stooks were moved to the green where the Maypole was, and all went home to get a few hours of sleep before the May Day festivities began.

I would like to make one small comment on this very modern attitude towards young people and their morals during the Beltane celebrations. When I was a young girl, I never saw a farm hand marry until his girlfriend was pregnant. In later years I asked my mother about this; she said the idea seemed to be that a girl had to prove herself fertile before marriage. Because country people needed children during those days (country children work very hard), a man and a girl needed to assure themselves of a family before they married.

SUMMER SOLSTICE/MIDSUMMER (June 21)

Summer Solstice was a very light and pretty festival. We would have lots of flowers and bird feathers, with some strewn on the ground.

Again, the Circle was eighteen feet wide, and both Tines were set up and decorated with flowers—gold coloured ones for the God, white ones for the Goddess. Bird nests were on the altar containing handmade artificial birds.

If it was warm enough not to have a fire, the altar was put in the middle of the circle with two lamps placed on it, one with a gold shade, and the other with a white one.

If the fire was lit the altar, of course, stayed in the North. Yellow and white flowers, kept in clear vases, were then used instead of the lamps.

Crystal goblets, filled with water, were placed in the quarters. Sometimes flower petals of the appropriate colours floated within them, with green leaves in the North. Irises decorated the altar and their leaves were woven into mats and placed underneath the vases.

Casting the Circle and calling the Quarters were as usual, and regardless of the phase of the moon, we would have a Drawing Down ceremony.

After the blessing of the cakes and wine, we danced in a very lighthearted fashion, but it was not Bacchanial, as May Eve was. Everyone waited for the sunrise, when the sun would be drawn down into a male Priest.

After this everyone left, except a Priest and Priestess (the two who had participated in both Drawing Down ceremonies), who then celebrated the Great Rite.

Incidentally, throughout this book I have referred to this Ritual as the "Great Rite" because it is generally called that nowadays, but in the olden times it was known simply as the Rite of Joining, or the Crossing Rite.

The origin of the expression, the Crossing Rite or, as some

Elders called it, the Ridencrux Rite, stems from very long ago, probably several hundred years in my estimation. This rite was enacted, so I was informed, in times of bad harvest and unseasonable weather. The High Priestess, on nights spanning from the New Moon to the Full Moon, would go to the nearest crossroads and wait for the first stranger travelling in the district. The Coven performed a ceremony beforehand, which is unknown now, to ensure that this traveller would be an embodiment of the God. Then the High Priestess performed the Great Rite with him to ensure that next season's sowing was successful.

I also believe that is how at one time they obtained the Corn King, who would be brought to the village and feted like a God until the appropriate time.

Crossroads are plentiful in the West Country; they all have names and there is a whole body of lore associated with them. Most magical charms have to be buried at a crossroads to be successful. Crossroads have very colourful names; the nearest one to where I lived was called Frogberry Cross which was associated with fertility charms. Strangely enough, I once had a pig, a sow, who always tried to get out and make her nest there to have her piglets. She had to walk about half a mile to reach it, but, on two occasions, she did manage it.

NOVEMBER EVE/SAMHAIN (Oct. 31)

Before I explain this Festival there is a small matter I would like to touch upon.

Many people today, most of whom have been converted to the Craft in the last ten years or so, have obviously been taught by those who were not in touch with any original Craft people. The word "Samhain" is pronounced, depending on the region one comes from, either "Sowin" or "Saveen." The word "Deosil", which means in a clockwise direction or going with the sun, is pronounced, "Jeshl."

I have not met anyone yet who knows this. Now, taking these mispronounciations in isolation, I could well be accused of "nit picking" but, coupled with this is a complete ignorance of the true meaning and importance of the ceremony of "Drawing Down the Moon".

I have met one experienced Craft woman who, in spite of being taught from latecomers' books, discovered by practical experience what momentous insight is gained from this ritual. She now works alone.

The majority of newcomers simply go through the motions, never experiencing the wonderful inner mystery of Wicca. This means, of course, that many of those whom these people teach leave the Craft again, as they do not receive the inner wisdoms and peace that comes from a truly spiritual experience. The particularly gifted few sometimes try again on their own, and happily find the secrets of the Hidden Path. But numerous individuals are disappointed and lost to the Craft forever.

In a world where there are more people than ever seeking an alternative to the Christian dogma, it is a very great pity that such a large number of true seekers end up believing there is nothing else but the physical plane of existence after all.

One final point: Witchcraft is a religion and a craft. The object of meeting once a month is twofold—to gain insight and spiritual strength from "Drawing Down", and to practice the craft side. We always worked in our Circle. If no person or animal in particular needed help, we used the power in a general way. But the power is raised to be used. That is the other criticism I have of some contemporary Wicca. Often no work is done at the Coven meeting.

Having said my piece, I will now explain November Eve.

Samhain was a reflective time, for it contained the essence of the old New Year.

Our Circle was eighteen feet with a portable forge in the centre, instead of a fire. Fires burned outside the Circle, at the quarters. Potatoes were put by these outside fires to be baked in embers later on.

Various produce was placed on the altar, such as fruit, vegetables, bread, etc. Corn Dollies also were present. A billhook (sickle), decorated with greenery, was carried by the Priest who

represented the God at the Festival and a decorated scythe stood at the side of the altar. Apples and nuts were at the quarters. Both Tines would be set up, and decorated with corn.

The Priest, with billhook, stayed outside the Circle and tended the fires. The High Priestess, carrying winnowed corn stalks was veiled. That year's May Queen wore strings of rose hips, had dried honesty pods in her hair, and carried hazel twigs.

There was a normal casting of the Circle and calling of the Quarters.

Immediately after the Quarters were called, a Priest and Priestess consecrated the cakes. The May Queen spoke:

> "We give thanks for the harvest, crops, and all living things.
> Urkay, Urkay, Mother Earth, we give thanks for thy bounty.
> Now is the season of the rest.
> Fallow lie the fields,
> Empty are the corn husks."

She crumbled a cake on the ground and poured a libation of wine. All danced round chanting,

> "Hartshorn and honeycomb, pippins shiny new,
> Berries black and rosy red, fresh and damp with dew.
> Oats and wheat and barley, wurzals, bean pods too,
> Jack o'lanterns golden, fennel, mint and rue.
> All are stored and gathered, safe from frost and mire,
> The harvest's in the granary, the cattle's in the byre."

When the chant was over, we passed wine once round. Then the High Priestess stood at the right of the altar, the May Queen on the left, and the rest of the women around the forge with their backs to it. The men then moved round the Circle, going with the sun, chanting:

> "Iron clad the meadows,
> Hoar frost covers all.
> Weasel slithers whitely,

Black rooks give call for call.
Fox shadows on the hillside,
Hunters Moon it swings on high,
The Wild Hunt is out now,
Winds through the chimney's sigh.
Herne comes a-walking
While the Lady takes her rest.
Loving, warm and gentle,
White dove within her nest.
Herne comes a-striding,
On Dolmen, Tor and hill,
Sees the hunter and the hunted,
In sky and field and rill.
Herne he comes a-leaping,
His Kingdom hard and cold,
But all are his own ones,
The frightened, shy or bold.
Herne he does his making,
His minding and his sending,
He cares for all in this Realm,
And in the next one, tending.
Death is but a doorway,
Herne is on both sides,
Here or there don't matter,
Old Herne with us abides."

While this was going on the Priest outside the Circle kept step with the chanting. In other words, he walked, then strode. He then cut a doorway and came leaping into the Circle, whereupon he sealed the doorway behind him.

As he entered the Circle, the May Queen moved from the side of the altar to join the others round the forge. The High Priestess stayed by the altar and the Priest presented her with the sickle. She threw back her veil, he gave her the Fivefold Salute and she then handed the sickle back to him.

Following this, the priest called for feasting. A doorway was cut and the potatoes that he had put in the embers before entering

the Circle were brought in. Rabbit was often cooked also—the only time that meat was ever eaten in a Circle. A cauldron, black inside and out, and filled with water would also be brought in and used as a Magic Mirror for scrying.

The men, as representatives of the God, were always very much in evidence around this Priest, and at the end of the ceremony, after the banishing, the God was welcomed by a male covenor.

YULE (Dec. 21)

Yule was generally celebrated among the Dolmens (Sarsen stones). Single, upright stones were called Dolmens, and those with a capstone were called Cromlechs.

If, for some reason, Yule was not celebrated among the standing stones, big logs would be used instead. Twelve were set upright around the edge of the Circle, and one in the middle of the fire. However, we usually managed to find a piece of upright granite for the centre of the fire. The Dolmens, or logs, were decorated with mistletoe and acorns.

As usual, the Circle was eighteen feet, with the normal Circle casting and calling of the Quarters. (Where I have not mentioned sweeping with the broom bundle, I have taken it for granted that the reader will assume this was always done.) After the Circle casting, and the calling of the Quarters, two Priests, dressed in black and brown and wearing masks with antlers, entered into the Circle through a doorway they cut and then resealed. The Priests, carrying fairly thick willow wands that had been stripped of bark, sprinkled salt and herbs around the Circle. Both circled and ended up face to face across the fire, while the High Priestess, dressed in brown and green, and her face veiled, stood in front of the altar.

Both men moved to face her, making gestures to claim her— beckoning, tugging her slightly, etc. The Priestess would appear puzzled, not knowing which one to turn to, and the two men would mock fight each other using the willow staves. One would go down, while the other stood over him and bent down to take the mask from his face. The vanquished one played dead, as in actual fact he was supposed to have been killed. As the victor pulled the mask from the "dead" one's face, it revealed a further mask underneath painted to resemble a skeleton.

The men carried the "dead" one off. (He returned unobtrusively, in ordinary Craft garb). The winner handed the High Priestess a sprig of mistletoe, and she would then remove her veil, go to the altar, and pick up a dish containing fish roe. She and the victor buried it near the East quarter of the fire.

All danced a ring dance, and then we had the Cakes and Ale Ceremony, followed by the banishing.

APPROPRIATE HERBS FOR SPECIFIC RITUALS

For purifying a magical working area: Hyssop, sage, tansy, valerian. These herbs may also be used in a ritual bath.

For Wiccanning: Lavender, also rosemary for protection.

For Handfasting: Marjorum, rosemary, yarrow.

Lady Day: Celandine, iris, tansy, violets.

May Eve: Marigold, meadowsweet, rose, woodruff.

Summer Solstice: Elder flowers, fennel, lavender, verbena.

November Eve: Mullein, sage, dried apple blossom.

Yule: Chamomile, pine, sage.

To purify and bless a new home: Basil, bay laurel, camphor. Hang up bunches of elder flowers, cowslips, rue. Plant a rowan tree.

ITEMS OF INTEREST
FROM THE OLD DAYS

CROSS ROAD CUSTOMS

If a young girl went to an appropriate crossroads on Midsummer night at midnight, she would meet her intended husband. A new silver coin could be "charged" in a Circle to attract success, and then buried at midnight at a crossroads on a waxing moon. For general good luck, a "charged" horseshoe could be buried at a crossroads, again at midnight on a waxing moon.

If you wished to meet a loved one who had passed on, you would go to the crossroads at midnight on November Eve and they would appear. If you desired to bring a couple together, you would make a charm of each of them, tie them together with ribbon and bury them at a crossroads at midnight on a full moon.

I found the following in a very old book when I was a teenager. I asked the owner of the book, which was handwritten by her, where she originally copied it from but, unfortunately, she could not remember.

"It is usual with many persons in South Devon, who are affected by agues, to visit at dead of night the nearest crossroads, five different times and there to bury a new laid egg.

The visit is paid about an hour before the cold fit is expected; and they are persuaded that, with the egg, they should bury the ague."

Four miles from where I lived, at a crossroads, was a monolith called the "Copplestone." It was squared and about twenty feet tall. Each of its four sides were about five feet wide at the base, but the stone narrowed as it went up. The monolith was of granite with very old carvings that archaeologists called "plaiting", which had been dated as being over one thousand years old.

The West Country is a popular holiday area, and as traffic increased, the Copplestone became a traffic hazard. Unless one literally hung out the car window, one could not see around it for oncoming traffic.

The local councillors decided to move the Copplestone. They told their workmen what they wanted done but not one of the Council employees would touch it, because each thought they would be cursed if the stone was touched. This story was reported as a newsworthy item by the local press back in the early 1960s. About three years later the local government officials tried once more to persuade the workmen to move the Copplestone and they finally agreed to move it six feet. Once more the press was in evidence, hoping, I expect, for some great supernatural calamity to befall the unfortunate workmen. The move was made, and in the hole where the Copplestone had stood were the fragile remains of a dagger. It is now in the local museum.

The removal of the stone has slightly eased the problem of clear vision when driving, to the extent that one now has to put only one's head right out of the car to see if anything is coming!

Country people, even in this day, are a conservative, traditional group of people.

SALUTING THE APPLE TREE

I remember an old custom connected with apple trees.

Apple orchards have always played a significant part in the every day life of the West Country as they are a vital part of the economy. Making cider from the apples to sell to local public houses, and to the big commercial cider companies, is an old and continuing part of rural economics.

Cakes were placed on the branches of an apple tree and cider was poured onto the roots while this rhyme was declaimed:

"Here's to thee, old apple tree.
Whence thou mayest bud, and whence thou mayest blow.
And when thou mayest bear apples enow!
Hats full! Caps full!
Bushel by bushel-sacks full,
And my pockets full too!
Hurrah-ya!"

This was a general custom, not a Wiccan one, but it has its origins in making a libation, if not to the Goddess, at least to the apple tree Guardian Spirit.

GENERAL PROTECTION FOR A HOUSE

For general protection for a house hang up white linen sachets containing equal amounts of rosemary and garlic.

Another protection that was considered very long lasting was to sprinkle iron filings around the house, going with the sun, and then covering them with earth. This was normally enacted when soil surrounded the house so that the filings were turned into the earth.

COUNTRY RITUALS AND BELIEFS

One of the ultimate "crimes" that was sure to bring the most dreadful bad luck was to burn bread. Even old crusts were never thrown into the fire. This was one of the earliest lessons we had to learn.

Food scraps were thrown out for the birds. Larger items were fed to livestock. Bread, or a handful of raw oatmeal, was placed underneath any plant that had to have a twig or leaves taken from it for magical workings.

Coins, to bring prosperity, were often buried under the front

doorstep. Good luck talismans were sometimes buried under the step, with the idea being that no one crossing the threshold could take the luck away from the people who lived in the house.

Simple "wishes" were written on a piece of paper by the elders of the village and then thrown on the fire. If the paper flew up the chimney, the wish would be granted.

THE BLIND DAYS

Years ago, the first three days of March were considered by Devon farmers to be the unlucky "blind days" and, on them, no farmer would sow any seed.

These days, often stormy (if March comes in like a lamb, it will go out like a lion, and vice versa), have been identified by some with the similarly ill-omened "borrowed days" of April.

These superstitions probably have their origins in the mists of antiquity and are likely the results of changes to the old calendar.

After all, "Samhain" originally meant "November".

STOKE GABRIEL CHURCH

The village of Stoke Gabriel, in South Devon, has a 13th century church.

The carvings around the door depict Gabriel; however on his right is carved Herne the Hunter, accompanied by a couple of his hounds.

THE WREN

A link with the Celts is seen in the local name of the little bird, the wren, which was considered a sacred bird by the Druids.

In Devonshire dialect it is known as "Cuddy Vran", which means "Bran's Sparrow".

THE DEVIL IN WIDECOMBE

On the evening of 21st October 1638, a rider, mounted on a jet black horse, entered the Poundstock Inn, asked his way to Widecombe and ordered a glass of ale.

The landlord's wife, who drew the ale, observed that it hissed and bubbled as it went down the rider's gullet.

She shrieked, and the Devil, for it was he no less, careened off, dashed into Widecombe church, seized an unfortunate boy asleep during the service, and disappeared with him through the roof.

Locals in the West still recount countless tales such as this one. Many are actually in written form, as many of the records, particularly church records, go back a long way.

MAY DAY

An old custom at Padstow in Cornwall was connected with May Day, the celebrations for which began at the stroke of midnight on the 30th of April.

Men and women would gather outside the inns, where they had eaten their supper together. Then, they would make their way around the town, singing,

> "Unite and unite, and let us all unite,
> For summer is a-coming unto day,
> And wither we are going we all will unite
> In the merry morning of May".

They would then rest for a few hours, until about ten in the morning when, once more gathering at the inn, the hobby horse was taken out into the street.

The "horse" was constructed from a black tarpaulin. It had a tall pointed cape, a ferocious face mask, flowing plumes, and savage looking jaws or "snappers".

In front of the man who carried it (he was hidden by the tarp) danced another dressed as a "fool" or jester. The jester held a painted club, composed of harmless layers of paper. He beat time to the music of the band with the club as they struck up the "Morning Song".

The other men who accompanied the hobby horse wore flowers in their hats. The doorways of the houses were decorated with green boughs which the young people had collected at dawn while they were "a-Maying".

All would frolic through the streets, while the horse made rushes at the crowd, snapping his jaws.

Minehead, in Somerset, had a similar May Morning ceremony. The "Morning Song" went as follows:

> "Robin Hood and Little John,
> They are both gone to Fair-O,
> And we will go to the merry greenwood
> To see what they do there-O.
> And for to choose-O
> To chase the buck and doe.
> With hal-an-tow (heel and toe)
> Jolly rumble-O
> For we were up as soon as any day-O
> And for to fetch the Summer home,
> The Summer and the May-O.
> For summer is a-come-O and winter is a-gone-O."

Their Harvest Supper at November Eve was called "Guldize". I cannot find the meaning of this word but "dize" has to do with the spinning of and decorating with flax; it is derived from the Anglo-Saxon "dise", meaning "bunch of flax on a distaff".

DUMPDEN HILL

Dumpden Hill, bordering the farm where I grew up, has a history of human habitation back to prehistoric times. Dumpden is one of those places with a lot of "atmosphere". It rises long and smooth from the fields and hedges at its feet. It looks artificial in the way Glastonbury Hill does, although both are creations of nature.

A popular story attached to Dumpden Hill is that, as the highest point in that part of the West, the Spanish Armada used it as a marker for navigation when they were sailing for Britain.

Dumpden also has a history of being used for rituals, and has a similarity of oddness that it shares with the Rollright Stones. (The Rollright stones are said to uncountable—each time they are counted, the number is different.)

At Dumpden Hill, mystery cloaks its crowning trees. There are reputed to be ninety-nine trees, but no two people have ever come up with the same number. However, if you ask a "local", they will tell you that Dumpden Hill does have ninety-nine trees.

FAIRY PATHS

A "Trod", or "Fairy Path", is a line seen in some fields that is a different shade of green to the rest. This is not to be confused with a "Fairy Ring", which is a circle of grass in a different shade of green.

The Trod goes in a completely straight line. I am of the opinion that a Trod is part of a Ley Line, and the magnetism affects the grass and therefore affects its hue. I have seen sheep jump a Trod rather than walk across it. Men would walk them if they were troubled with rheumatism.

HORSES

A strange superstition concerning horses and their hooves was quite prevalent in the west. (Horses, being sacred to the Goddess, would have received excellent care.)

When a Blacksmith trimmed a horse's hooves, he gathered all

the trimmings and threw them upon the fire. It was considered unlucky to leave them about, or to throw them away.

They probably viewed the trimmings in a similar fashion to people's finger nails, which can be magically used against a person. I do recall that it was supposed to be possible to use the parings to make the horse throw its rider.

Gypsies used horse hoof parings to entice dogs, as dogs love them! The superstition could, of course, have something to do with that mysterious group known as "Horse Whisperers". Gypsies were sometimes "Horse Whisperers", and even today a thriving group of this equine secret shamanistic society is reputed to exist somewhere in Britain.

THE CHEESEWRING

The Cheesewring on Bodmin Moor, Cornwall, is a strange lump of granite. Its odd shape is believed to be of natural formation, which has been weathered into its present form.

A legend speaks of a Druid with a gold cup who lived near the Cheesewring. It was impossible to empty this cup, and the Druid offered it to thirsty travellers passing by. One who tried unsuccessfully to empty it, rode off with the cup in a fit of rage. His horse fell over the rocks, the man was killed and the cup buried with him.

This sounds like yet another tall story of the West Country. But, in 1818, a nearby cairn known as King Arthur's grave, was opened and in it was found a gold cup dating around 1500 B.C.

It is generally believed that the Cheesewring, and Bowerman's Nose on Dartmoor, along with other great stones, are the remnants of some vast, interrelated power storage temples. The temples of Cornwall were to heal the body, and those in Devon for refreshing the spirit.

Cornish women, many years after the rest of England was Christian, were, after a successful confinement, still placing the placenta at the foot of a Menhir to thank the Goddess for their successful delivery. The placenta was also a sign to the Gods that the delivery was a happy one.

WISH HOUNDS

On Dartmoor, the Hounds of the Wild Hunt were known as "Wish Hounds". I can remember my grandmother saying to me, when she wanted me to be quiet, "Hold your wish".

I have wondered ever since if it had anything to do with the Hounds. In North Devon they are called "Yeth" or "Yell" Hounds, that is "Heath Hounds", or "Heathen Hounds".

THE HEARTH STONE AND THE HEARTH FIRE

Originally the Hearth Stone was a small edition of an upright standing stone that stood next to the fire and contained the Hearth Spirit.

It was considered very bad luck to let the domestic fire go out, as the hearth and its stone were the centre point, the heart of the house. Even in my time, country people did not like the fire being allowed to go out. As long as there was a spark or two in the fireplace in the morning that would "catch", they were happy.

As a general rule, the kitchen fire, which they cooked on, was the most important fire.

On the rare occasions that the morning fire appeared dead, every means was tried to relight it, except paper and matches. If it had to be re-laid, and paper used, it was admitting that the hearth was "cold", and was looked upon as bringing bad luck.

THE RIVER GOD

I remember an old Devon saying, "River of Dart, River of Dart, every year thou claimest a heart." (The River Dart is the main river in Devon.) I believe an old custom of putting blood in the river, along with seeds and metal, was to propitiate the river god as much as anything.

CELTIC INVOCATION

The following is an Ancient Celtic Invocation (re-phrased into modern English):

"I will pluck the smooth yarrow stalk,
That my figure may be sweeter,
My lips warmer, my voice full of rejoicing.
May my voice be like a sunbeam,
My lips like the juice of strawberries.
I would be an Island in the sea,
A hill on the land, a star in the dark time,
A staff to the weak one.
I shall wound every man,
And be hurt by none."

UNRAVELING MYTH AND LORE

To discover the origins of the Old Religion, or even to try and understand it, one must look at Celtic history, Irish and Welsh mythology and surviving remnants of folklore which are still practiced.

Within myth is hidden a grain of truth. It was belief in this concept that led to the discovery of Troy.

It is very difficult, of course, to find one thread that starts now and runs back clearly to some past belief. It is rather like trying to untangle a very jumbled ball of wool. King Arthur is a prime example.

In King Arthur we have a 5th or 6th Century tribal chief who held back the Saxons, and possibly to a lesser degree also fought the Romans in the west. When he died people did not want to think he had gone forever—a very natural reaction even today.

(One has only to think of those who do not believe President Kennedy is dead or, for that matter, Elvis Presley.)

The tribal King Arthur, therefore, became merged with a Celtic God in people's minds.

That is one very basic start of an unravelling. Malory enlarged on the Arthurian tales and brought them into the Age of Chivalry, with its Knights and Ladies. Then he added Norman French Romances, including the personage of Lancelot du Lac.

However, if one looks at the triangle of Arthur, Lancelot and Guinevere, one can see an older story behind them; the story of Blodeuwedd, Lleu Llaw Gyffes and Gronw. Apparently, both of the names Blodeuwedd and Guinevere, mean "Owl" or "Flower-face".

So it would seem, then, that one of the threads goes back to an older, Celtic version of wife, husband and lover. The similarity is, of course, reinforced by the fact that both wives were chosen for their husbands, without any personal say in the matter, and that when the husband's best friend is introduced, the wife falls in love with him, and he with her.

If one takes the story back one more step, we have the triangle between the Goddess, the God of the Waxing year, and the God of the Waning year. This duality of God forms is quite common in the majority of Celtic traditions of the Craft.

The unravelling of threads by means of myth and folklore is fascinating, but frustrating. A good deal of time and patience is required and then, more often than not, the threads break and we have to start over again.

The difficulties are compounded by the fact that dialects also alter the meaning of words, and so does the difference in the language spoken today as compared to that of someone in Chaucer's time.

A simple example is the London District and Public House known as the "Elephant and Castle". Originally this was the "Infanta of Castille" but the constant repetition over the years through Cockney dialect has completely changed the name.

A phrase common nowadays, "So Mote it Be" is most likely another example of words and phrases being misheard and be-

coming scrambled. The original was "Motte Ye" but, to the best of my knowledge, it has nothing to do with the Craft.

Another simple example is the expression, or rather expletive, "Bloody". This started out as "By-the-Lady!"; quite a pleasant emphasis of speech, in fact. The Lady in question, while viewed by most as meaning the Virgin Mary, must in reality be, of course, none other than the Goddess.

Yet another instance of misunderstanding, through lack of old knowledge, is that pertaining to the "Witches Broom". The Broom used in the Circle was not A broom, the household article, but SOME broom, i.e. some twigs from the bush or shrub whose common name is "Yellow Broom".

I am often amused at the antics of some present day witches here with their brooms. They have appeared on television, prancing and leaping round the television studio, on great broom sticks, to demonstrate what Wicca is about!

In resolving this misinterpretation, it is important, too, to realize that anything said at the witch trials was most probably false, especially since many of the unfortunate people murdered as witches, were, in fact, not of the Craft.

Also, during the trails, genuine witches hid the true meaning of their religion. There is never a mention of the Goddess, for example. Witches were quite willing to admit to worshipping the devil, and having intercourse with him, because they knew that was what the inquisitors wanted to hear, while it also kept their true beliefs secret. Witches, of course, do not believe in the devil.

So they satisfied their torturors, and STILL kept their beliefs hidden.

But, of course, in small communities, some of their conversations would have been overheard, and probably misheard. That is why witches would have been as guarded with their speech as they were with the tools of the Craft. One example was the use of everyday objects such as a knife and cup, so that their significance would not be obvious.

From misunderstandings such as this the mythology of the "witch's broom" evolved. Of course witches would admit flying to a Sabbat on a broom, because this was not what it meant.

Witches did use some hallucinogenic herbs, without a doubt. I have been told they were often given to new witches to confuse them, so that they would not be able to tell anyone who was at the Sabbat, and where it was held.

I do not think the use of these drugs was widespread among experienced witches, for if they were in a drugged state they would not have been in a condition to participate fully in the Drawing Down the Moon.

I cannot see that witches who knew they could reach an altered state of consciousness without recourse to drugs would have used drugs very much in any but a curative way, such as for relieving pain, etc.

I believe that the admission to the inquisitors that drugs were used to hallucinate was another "blind", as they would not have wanted anyone outside the Craft to have knowledge of what an incredible experience the Drawing Down ceremony is.

Broom was a slang kind of euphemism for a woman's genitals. "Riding a witches broom" was, again, an earthy euphemism for ritual copulation. It is as simple as that. In some parts of England it is still looked on as extremely bad taste to leave a house broom propped up outside one's cottage or house near the lane or road. The backyard is the place for it, or the kitchen. A broom displayed at the front of the house meant, and still means, that the lady of the house is open for business, in a trade of the oldest profession—prostitution!

Returning to the subject of unravelling threads from the past, the most fascinating thread I have encountered over the years is the similarity between quite diverse religious philosophies.

The Japanese martial and spiritual art of Ninjutsu, Chinese Taoism, and Tibetan Mysticism, all have the same basic tenets as Wicca.

The Ninjas use a five pointed star for the four elements and one they call "Void", or "Spirit".

Taoism, basically a nature religion, is, of course, based on the polarity of male and female.

Tibetan Mystics use an upturned bell as a cup, and place in it

a short wand.

The above is an oversimplification, of course, but to explain the similarities in detail would require a book in itself.

It is as if each philosophy has a piece of the same jigsaw puzzle, and whether there are still pieces missing, I do not know. I see it as a tree with many branches, all emanating from the one trunk, with different branches appealing to different people.

MERRY MEET AND MERRY PART, AND MERRY MEET AGAIN.

Our traditional greeting and goodbye was "Merry Meet" for "Hello", and "Merry Part and Merry Meet again", for "Goodbye." I do not know where the greeting "Blessed Be" started, but it was probably instigated by Gerald Gardner.

Having arrived at the end of my notes, I realise this is a very slim volume in comparison with other books on the Old Religion.

However, to the best of my knowledge, I have omitted nothing of any importance. That is, the Rituals are complete. I cannot lengthen them, or add any that we did not celebrate.

If I offend any reader by comments made within these pages, I can only say that the Craft to me is of paramount importance.

While I realize the Craft must change and grow, the spiritual significance of its inner truths must not be lost, or we shall simply have a Mummers Play — a curiosity that the community knows is enacted but whose significance and inner meaning are forgotten.

The revival of an interest in the countryside, and the movement of people away from the cities, is the most helpful sign in this age for the continued survival of the Craft.

It does not require large numbers to participate in this migration, but the caring minority that I have met here and in Britain are all that is needed for the love of this planet to grow.

The Craft is not for everyone and I do not think it will ever have large numbers of adherents in this age of the world. All it needs is the compassionate few who rejoice in the simple, natural things that our planet offers to all and which enriched my childhood so greatly.

It is difficult to express in words the feeling of continuity that stems from engaging in the Art, in a place that has seen the Rites for years uncountable.

In the early morning of a summer's day, the dew glints on countless spider's webs in the hedgerows. They are spread like a diamond-studded cloak of lace across the living green, as if woven in the realms of Faery.

The old, cobwebby magic of the Craft is felt in granite stone, standing like a sentinel on the wild moors. It is echoed in the waving fields of corn as summer dies, and in the ringing note of the Blacksmiths hammer as the breath of horse and man drifts mistily on a chill winter's morning.

The feeling that there is a place for everything and everything is in its allotted place, whether grasses, flowers, insects, animals or man, permeates the country dweller's existence.

In the quiet, green places, where I grew, it is very simple to realise that just beyond sight, almost at the corner of one's eye, can be perceived Merlin's Isle of Gramarye and the Isles of the Blest. Never changing, always changing, and within reach of those who truly care and who can see the hand of the God and Goddess in everything they perceive.

OLD COUNTRY RECIPES

SCENTED CANDLES

Beeswax alone can be used for candles, or a mixture of beeswax and paraffin wax. Beeswax is a golden brown colour, so if you wish to colour candles made from pure beeswax, this has to be taken into account. Wax crayons, melted with the wax, are the easiest method of obtaining coloured candles.

A few aromatic fresh herbs, perhaps rosemary, lavender or lemon verbena, can be immersed in the melted wax and kept at a temperature below 180°F for forty-five minutes. Dried herbs can be added to the melted wax so that the candles are flecked with herbs.

Wicks can be bought from handicraft shops, or fine waxed string can be used as a substitute.

Moulds can be made from cardboard tubes with one end covered, or yogurt containers, shampoo containers, etc. (Don't forget to thread the wick through first.) Moulds should be lightly oiled with cooking oil before use.

It is important to melt wax slowly, either in a double saucepan or in a container over a pan of hot water. Keep the heat low; never let wax bubble.

DRIED HERBS FOR USE INSTEAD OF INCENSE

Lavender   Suitable for Midsummer Festival
and Handfasting

Rosemary	A herb of protection
Marjorum	Venus herb, suitable for Handfastings
Thyme	A protective herb; used to invoke Fairy Folk
Lemon Verbena	A herb of inspiration and protection
Bay	A herb of love
Basil	A fertility herb
Mint	A herb of success
Geraniums	A herb of healing
Meadow sweet	A herb for marital happiness
Tansy	A herb particularly associated with the Goddess
Myrtle	A herb of love and fertility

SPICES

Cinnamon	Used for purifying
Cloves	Enhances psychic ability
Mace	Aids concentration
Fennel	Used for consecrating ritual weapons
Nutmeg	Strengthens clairvoyance
Coriander	Love and peace

All plants should be gathered before they are fully open, on a dry day. Petals and leaves should be dried as quickly as possible, but away from the sunlight. A warm, dry, airy room is ideal. Herbs can be hung up in small bunches, but the air must be able to circulate all round them. Flowers can be dried on kitchen paper, with another sheet laid lightly over the top. Drying time will depend on the weather and type of plant. Do not dry too large a quantity at once as the virtue will go out of them after three months. Store all herbs in air-tight jars, until ready for use.

To find a scent which is pleasing, experiment with two or three different combinations.

HERBS FOR STREWING

While no one nowadays strews their floor with aromatic leaves and flowers, some might like to strew a Circle, particularly for a Handfasting.

In the 16th century the following herbs were very popular for strewing: Balm, camomile, cowslips, daisies, fennel, lavender, marjorum, roses, sage, tansy, violet, lemon balm, bay and basil.

Thomas Tusser, who died in 1580, was a farmer noted for his observations of farming practices in Suffolk and Norfolk. He wrote:

> "While wormwood hath seed,
> Get a bundle or twain,
> To save against March,
> To make flea refrain:
> Where chamber is swept,
> And wormwood is strown,
> No flea for his life,
> Dare abide to be known."

This can be a useful herb for those of us with pet cats or dogs.

DEVONSHIRE CREAM

This is the traditional cream of the District and is known as "clouted" cream, or "clotted" cream. It has to be made with milk straight from the cow and, of course, Jersey cows give the richest milk of all.

Allow a gallon of milk to stand in a pan for several hours, then heat extremely slowly until small rings are formed on the surface. The pan should be put in a cool place for twenty-four hours and the cream then skimmed off.

SABBAT CAKE RECIPE

Four ounces of butter
Two eggs
One tablespoon of honey
Two tablespoons of cream
Six ounces wholemeal flour
Half teaspoon cinnamon or mixed spice

Method One:

Cream butter and honey, beat in eggs and cream. Fold in flour and spice. Cut into crescents and bake in a moderate oven for about ten minutes. When cool, dust with icing sugar, or cinnamon and nutmeg.

Method Two:

Rub butter into flour and spice. Add beaten eggs, honey and cream. Cut into crescents and bake in a moderate oven for about ten minutes. When cool, dust with icing sugar, or cinnamon and nutmeg.

MEAD RECIPE

3 pounds honey
2 egg whites
1 ounce of yeast
1 lemon
1 gallon of cold water

Put honey and grated rind from the lemon in a large saucepan or preserving pan with the gallon of cold water. Beat the two egg whites until frothy and add to the other ingredients in the pan. Place the pan over heat and stir as mixture comes to boil. Simmer gently for one hour. Pour liquid into a large bowl and leave until lukewarm, then stir in the yeast. Cover bowl and leave in a warm place for three days. Stir daily. Then strain through muslin and bottle. Cork loosely. Push corks down gradually as fermentation ceases. Store bottles in a cool, dark place.

The mead will be ready to drink in one year.

METHEGLIN RECIPE

5 pounds of honey
1 gallon of water
1 lemon
1 sprig of rosemary
1 sprig of balm
3/4 ounce of yeast

Simmer the herbs and thinly sliced lemon rind for twenty minutes in the gallon of water.

Strain the liquid and pour onto the honey, stirring well. When lukewarm, add the juice of the lemon and the yeast. Cover and leave for twenty-four hours, then stir and leave in a warm place until fermentation ceases.

Strain the mead into bottles and keep them in a cool, dark place for one year.

BLACKBERRY WINE

3 pounds of blackberries
3 pounds of sugar
1 gallon of boiling water

Wash berries, put in a large bowl and pour over them the gallon of boiling water. Stir well, then cover the bowl and leave for ten days. Strain liquid through muslin, add the three pounds of sugar and stir well. Cover the bowl and leave for three days, but stir daily.

Put into bottles and cork, loosely at first.

The wine will be ready to drink in six months.

ROSE-HIP WINE

3 pounds of rose hips
3 pounds of sugar
1 gallon of boiling water

Wash the rose hips and cut them in half. Put them in a large bowl and pour on the gallon of boiling water. Stir well with a wooden spoon, then cover the bowl and leave for two weeks. After this time, strain off the liquid into another bowl and add the 3 pounds of sugar. Stir till sugar is dissolved, then cover the bowl and leave for five days, stirring daily.

Bottle, remembering to cork loosely at first, and store in a cool, dark place. Push in corks when wine has finished fermenting.

It will be ready to drink in six months.

DANDELION WINE

2 quarts dandelion flowers
3 pounds sugar
1 ounce yeast
1 lemon
1 orange
1 gallon boiling water

Pick the dandelions on a sunny day. Pick just the heads until you have two quart jugs full. Wash the flowers and put them in a large bowl.

Slice the orange and lemon thinly and add to the flower-heads. Pour the gallon of boiling water over them, and stir well. Cover the bowl and leave for ten days, but no longer. Strain the liquid into another bowl and stir in the 3 pounds of sugar. Spread the ounce of yeast on a piece of toast, and float on top.

Cover the bowl and leave for another 3 days. Remove the

toast, strain again, and bottle, again corking loosely at first. The wine will be ready to drink in three months.

TEA WINE

4 pints cold tea
2 pounds sugar
1 pound raisins
2 lemons

Cut up the raisins, slice the lemons thinly and put both in a large bowl. Add 2 pounds of sugar, then pour on the four pints of cold tea. Stir until the sugar has dissolved, then cover the bowl and leave for a month.

After this time you will a find thin mould on the top. Remove this, then strain liquid and bottle.

Keep in a cool, dark place, remembering to cork lightly at first.

This is ready in one month but it is much nicer if you keep it for six months before drinking.

OLD COUNTRY REMEDIES

WINE REMEDIES

Cowslip wine will cure jaundice.

Dandelion wine is good for kidney troubles and indigestion.

Sloe wine is effective for diarrhea.

Elderberry wine taken on a hot or cold morning will ward off colds.

Raspberry wine is invaluable for sore throats.

Blackcurrant wine, mulled, is excellent for colds and bronchitis.

Barley wine is good for kidney troubles.

Celery tea is good for rheumatism. Boil a few stalks of celery in a pint of water for about half an hour, then strain off the liquid. Drink a glass every day. Sufferers from rheumatism should not drink rhubarb wine.

HERBAL REMEDIES—MEDICINAL

IRIS ROOT—Boiled, is an antiseptic solution.

CLOVER—Boiled in a little water and then the water is used to stimulate the heart.

POWDERED HOPS—Calms and promoted sleep.

LADY'S MANTLE—Infusion for the treatment of acne.

PLANTAIN—Whole plant can be used for catarrh and worms; fresh leaves crushed for wounds, sores and insect bites.

PARSLEY—A tea made from crushed parsley seeds, kills

head lice. (It is of course put on the hair and not ingested.)

MINT – A tea made from mint is good for cramps, migraine, heartburn and nausea.

YELLOW DOCK – Use root. One teaspoon to one cup of water is a mild laxative and blood purifier. Useful as an ointment for itching, sores, swollen insect bites. Can also be used on boils. To make an ointment, mix an infusion of yellow dock root with hot lard.

WOUNDWORT – Useful as a wash for wounds. Can be used as a gargle, and as a wash for thrush. It is also a worm expellent.

HONEY – Honey must be the most wonderful substance ever put here for our use. Wrap burns in a honey soaked bandage. The same treatment is used for blisters. It heals cuts and wounds, and is a natural antiseptic. Rubbed well in the skin until all stickiness has vanished it will improve texture of skin and assist in keeping skin youthful.

CHEST COLDS

1 tablespoon aniseed
2 tablespoons lungwort
2 tablespoons coltsfoot

COUGHS

6 chopped white onions
Half a cup of honey

Put onions and honey in a double boiler. Cook for two hours. Strain. Take at regular intervals, warm.

BRONCHIAL COUGH

2 tablespoons coltsfoot
2 tablespoons horehound
1 tablespoon cherry bark

Simmer in two and a half cups of water for twenty minutes. Strain, add honey to sweeten. Take two to four tablespoons 4 times a day.

HEAD COLDS

2 tablespoons comfrey
2 tablespoons angelia
2 tablespoons horehound
1 tablespoon mugwort
1 tablespoon nettle
1 tablespoon peppermint

Infuse in half a pint of water and drink as required, warm.

A USEFUL LINIMENT

7 tablespoons oil of camphor
2 tablespoons oil of cloves
3 tablespoons oil of wintergreen
3 tablespoons oil of eucalyptus

Shake well before use.

FOR RELIEF OF VARICOSE VEINS

Equal amounts of:
Sweet flag root
Nettle leaves
Thyme leaves
Horsechestnut leaves and fruit

Boil in one quart of water. Cool, and add half a teaspoon sea or rock salt. Bathe legs.

ASTHMA

1 each, dried:
Garlic
Blackthorn
Blue vervain

Simmer in one quart of water for twenty minutes, strain. Take one dessert spoon, four times daily.

SOME COUNTRY REMEDIES

When I was a child, if a farmhand cut himself he would go to the barn and take a handful of cobwebs from the rafters to put in the cut. The cobweb acted like a very fine dressing and staunched the bleeding.

One old lady in the village always kept a small amount of jam at the bottom of the jampot. When a child got a septic wound or spot, she put the mould that had formed on the jam on the infected area. This was, of course, long before the advent of penicillin.

If jam wouldn't set while being made, or butter when being churned, the person making them would say as they stirred, "Here is some for old Mrs. Such and Such, and here is some for old Mr. So and So." They would go through all the names of the oldest people in the village. I heard the explanation for this being given to an "outsider" once, and when the villager had finished explaining that it was a sort of charm to make the jam or butter go right, she turned to me and said, "'Tis only a bit of Witchcraft entit, after all". This was their attitude to the Craft; that it was extraordinary in an ordinary, everyday sort of way. It was part of the unseen world that acted upon the seen, even in very mundane matters.

HERBAL REMEDIES—COSMETIC

To improve the complexion wash with rainwater. Instead of soap, use a mixture of finely ground oatmeal, ground almonds and finely ground orange peel. If the skin is dull looking or spotty, use sugar mixed with soap lather, and rinse with water that has lemon juice in it. Try the treatment for one week.

CLEANSING MASKS

1) Equal parts powdered yeast, oatmeal and yogurt.
2) A cup of buttermilk, simmered for half an hour, with a handful of elderflowers steeped in it.
3) Strawberry cleansing mask: Mash up three or four large strawberries, and smear on the face. Leave for about ten minutes and rinse off with rose water.
4) Mayonnaise makes an excellent skin softener, if you don't mind the idea of putting it on your face!

SKIN TONICS

Rose water is an excellent skin tonic.

Recipe for rose water: Take three handfuls of red rose petals, picked in the morning, before the sun is strong. Put them in two pints of rainwater in an earthenware oven dish with a lid. Heat an oven to 450°F and bring water to boiling point. Simmer for fifteen minutes. Cool and strain. If the scent is not strong enough, add again the same amount of rose petals, and repeat.

Marigold water, made in similar fashion, is good for troubled, spotty skin.

Elder flower water keeps the skin free from blemishes.

Dandelion water is good for a sallow skin.

Yarrow is healing and astringent.

Cucumber juice and witchhazel is an astringent for enlarged pores.

A good quick toner before going out to a party, for example, is egg white. It tightens the skin and temporarily reduces wrinkles.

The egg yolk can be mixed with ordinary shampoo to give an extra gloss to the hair.

HERBAL BATHS

Rosemary, lemon balm and meadowsweet all relieve tired limbs and aching muscles.

Lavender is refreshing and a natural disinfectant.

Blackberry leaves are invigorating.

Chamomile is very soothing and relaxing.

Plantain leaves can be used for skin ailments.

Lovage is a natural deodorant.

Elder leaves and flowers are healing and stimulating.

Lime flowers are very calming.

Mugwort relieves tiredness.

Bay leaves comfort an ache in the limbs.

HAIR CARE

An infusion of rosemary makes an excellent hair rinse for dark hair. Use chamomile, or yarrow and chamomile, for fair hair.

Blackberry leaves and sage leaves, either infused or boiled together, help keep dark hair from going grey.

Thyme and rosemary, infused together, help to prevent dandruff.

An infusion of nettles is also a preventative for dandruff. If dandruff is already present, a strong infusion of nettles, mixed with four tablespoons of cider vinegar, will help to get rid of it.

For thinning hair, slice a large onion in half a cup of rum and leave for twenty-four hours. Strain. Massage some of that liquid into the scalp every night for a week. Repeat, using it twice a week for the remainder of one month.

A SUMMARY OF SOME HERBS AND THEIR USES:

Antiseptic: Lavender, thyme, peppermint, wintergreen.
Astringent: Sage, milfoil, nettle.
Calming: Balm, marjoram, valerian, hops.
Cleansing: Lovage, milfoil, lemongrass, geranium leaves.
Healing: Milfoil, rosemary, lovage; the flowers of: Chamomile, elder, linden.
Moisturizing: Chamomile flowers, rose petals and leaves, white willow bark.
Stimulating: Thyme, rosemary, lavender.
Toning: Thyme, lavender, milfoil, nettle.

An infusion of herbs is similar to making a pot of tea. Put the herbs in a bowl, pour boiling water on them, leave until warm, strain and use.

OTHER HERBAL USES

Sleep pillows, aids to a good night's sleep, have become very popular again in recent times. Mix equal quantities of dried hops and cowslips in a pillow.

Lavender and rose petals are soothing in a sick room. They can be mixed in equal parts, with half the quantity of lemon verbena added, and a small handful of dried rosemary.

Mugwort, mixed with some more aromatic herbs, such as bay, marjorum, rosemary and lavender, is reputed to aid in prophetic dreams.

Herbs for clothes drawers: Feverfew keeps most insects away. Tansy keeps away fleas. Woodruff deters moths. Rosemary is also a moth deterrent. Lavender is probably the best known and most traditional herb for putting among linen.

Whenever herbs are made into pillows or sachets for drawers, a good pinch of dried orris root mixed with the herbs will help to preserve their perfume.

METHODS OF DIVINATION

DIVINATION USING 36 ORDINARY PLAYING CARDS.

Ace of Hearts - The home; reversed, a troubled home.

Two of Hearts - Two of time (two days, weeks, months), or news from loved ones.

Three of Hearts - Three in time (three days, weeks, or months).

Four of Hearts - Very minor difficulties to overcome.

Six of Hearts —New found happiness, or new found whatever the card is next to.

Seven of Hearts —New romantic happiness, a new love affair.

Eight of Hearts —Happiness, love and fulfillment; long lasting.

Nine of Hearts —Wish fulfillment card.

Ten of Hearts —A social occasion, a special outing.

Jack of Hearts —A young man, husband, lover, son, brother, or a fair-haired young man with blue eyes.

Queen of Hearts —A fairhaired woman with blue eyes.

King of Hearts —An older man with fair hair and blue eyes.

Ace of Diamonds —A surprise gift; with other diamonds, a gift of money.

Seven of Diamonds —New money from a business source.

Eight of Diamonds —Money.

Nine of Diamonds —Unexpected money.

Ten of Diamonds —Travel; with Ace of Diamonds, a gift of money.

Jack of Diamonds —A young man, auburn hair, grey eyes.

Queen of Diamonds —A woman, auburn or grey hair, grey eyes.

King of Diamonds —An older man, auburn or grey hair, grey eyes.

Ace of Clubs — A message or letter; if reversed, a personal message, i.e. delivered in person.

Seven of Clubs — Whatever this card is next to will happen quickly.

Eight of Clubs — Confusion over subject matter of reading.

Nine of Clubs — Adds certainty to whatever reading is about.

Ten of Clubs — Long journey.

Jack of Clubs — Young man, dark hair, blue eyes.

Queen of Clubs — Dark haired, blue eyed woman.

King of Clubs — An older man, dark hair, blue eyes.

Ace of Spades — An official or government building; reversed, an official message or document.

Seven of Spades — Movement, either in a person's life or a physical moving (changing homes).

Eight of Spades — Setbacks or minor health problems.

Nine of Spades — Delays and disappointments.

Ten of Spades — Dishonesty, or warnings of deception.

Jack of Spades — A dark haired, dark eyed young man.

Queen of Spades — A dark haired, dark eyed woman.

King of Spades — An older man, dark haired, dark eyed.

Where blue eyes are suggested, they may be grey or green.

Sometimes the King and Queen of Hearts represent those tied by emotional bonds, either married couples, or parents and children.

The King of Clubs can represent a business man; the King of Spades can represent a lawyer; the King of Diamonds can represent an official of some kind.

The cards have, of course, to be read in groups. The more they are used, the more meanings you will find in them, and the more deeply you will be able to interpret them.

An appropriate card is selected for the querant. A young man under about thirty-five, with dark hair and blue or grey eyes, would be the Jack of Clubs. Card one is the querant. The cards are laid out as follows:

(3,8,13,18,23,28,33)
(1,2,7,12,17,22,27,32)
(5,10,15,20,25,30,35)   (6,11,16,21,26,31,36)
(4,9,14,19,24,29,34)

It will be seen that the cards are laid by putting number two card next to the querant, then the third card laid is put in the top section, the fourth card laid in the bottom section, the fifth in the left hand row and the sixth in the right hand row, then back to the middle row for card number seven, and so on, until all the cards are laid. The cards are shuffled by the querant before commencing, but after the querant card has been removed. They are generally laid face up.

The middle row, with the querant card in it, relates to the current situation and describes events happening in the present.

The left hand row is the past; the bottom row consists of environmental factors affecting the querant; the top row represents immediate probabilities which may occur very soon; the right hand row concerns the future.

RUNE STONES

Rune stones have become very popular in recent times. The fact that they have magical working properties as well is an added attraction.

There are many books around now explaining how to use these stones for either divination or magical workings. I will not, therefore, go over ground that is covered by more learned Runesters than myself, but will give their more esoteric meanings and relate them to the Trumps Major of the Tarot. (Tarot cards were known in my time as "Gypsy Cards".)

I will refer to them mostly by names that are in use at the present time and in the form that covers the majority of modern Runes.

If one looks at the Rune stones or the Trumps Major as a learning device and not simply as a divinatory tool, the Path to follow is from the highest number to the lowest, or in the case of the Tarot Trumps, from the highest number to zero.

The lower the number, the more spiritual the Runes and Tarot become. Rune stones can, of course, be used as "Astral Doorways", as can the Tarot Trumps. I have found with the Runes that while meditating with the symbols to gain information about the Runes themselves, I have received wisdom and guidance for myself. Those I teach have had similar experiences. This is, of course, valuable and illuminating but I am still trying to learn about the pre-history of the Runes.

FEHU – Mobile force, power, energy, fertility, becoming.
URUZ – Formulates, (Cosmic Seed), origins and destiny.
THURISAZ – Instinctual will; destruction and defence.
ANSUZ – Transformer/Expressor of spiritual power and knowledge.
RAIDO – Archetypal law and order; the Cosmic Wheel.
KENAZ – Mankind; the making of three from two.
GEBO – Psychic joining together; man to man; gods to gods.
WUNJO – Fellowship and goodwill.
HAGALAZ – Eternal Cosmic harmony.
NAUTHIZ – Concept of stepping forward into manifestation; "Needfire" created by friction.
ISA – The force that holds the ego-self together during stressful trials, such as Initiation.
JERA – Fruition of efforts well spent.
EIHWAZ – Life giving force and mode by which that life is sustained.
PERTHRO – Constant change that is always the same.
ALGUZ – Power of human spirit; striving towards the world of the gods.
SOWELU – Spiritual force that guides the Initiate towards the goal.
TIWAZ – The world and cosmic order through balance.
BERKANA – The Great Mother.

EHWAZ—Symbol of ideal man/woman relationship.
MANNAZ—Initiation of blood brotherhood.
LAGUZ—Basic life energy.
INGWAZ—The Great Father.
DAGAZ—Synthesis of the powers of day and night; polarity.
OTHALA—Material prosperity and well being.

THE TAROT TRUMPS

While the Tarot is obviously from an age long before Christianity, it does suffer in some ways from what I call a "Christianising" of some of the cards.

No one now knows what the originals looked like, but recent artists have tried gradually to correct this, for the benefit of the cards in general, and for their use as a divinatory tool in particular.

The overlaying of Christian symbology has altered the meaning of those in question. The three cards I refer to are:

THE DEVIL. It has become a very negative card, when it should really represent the earthly plane and the life force. Now, if one is a slave to materialism, or sexual gratification without love, then the card IS negative. But it basically deals with matters on the earthly plane.

JUDGEMENT. This is a card of re-birth. It can be seeing daylight at the end of the tunnel, if it applies to a situation where the consultant of the cards has had an extremely torrid time, or it can be concerned with spiritual enlightenment.

THE HIEROPHANT. Usually depicted as the Pope, or an authoritive figure, with very Christian regalia. This card represents man, spiritually whole and triumphant; a card of spiritual attainment and enlightenment. This is the great leap Ceremonial Magicians strive for when working their way up the Kabbalistic Tree. It can also be a reminder, in divination, for the person to listen to their inner voices or, on a mundane level, to take advice from those of greater wisdom.

0 *THE FOOL*—Pure spirit. "Nirvana". The zero which contains all.

1 *MAGICIAN*—Mercury, messenger of the Gods. Balance and skill in the magical arts. An Adeptus.

2 *HIGH PRIESTESS*—Highest aspect of all femininity, Veiled Isis. Female counterpart to the Magician.

3/4 *EMPRESS/EMPEROR*—The highest aspects attainable, before the Veil.

5 *HIEROPHANT*—Guide on the inner planes to enable travellers to attain the highest levels.

6 *LOVERS*—Recognition of higher self. Male and female in harmony. Perfection, with the world still unrealised.

7 *CHARIOT*—Triumph with balance. The equilibrium of Spirit and Matter in harmony.

8 *JUSTICE*—The inner balance needed in this world to enable one to listen to...the Hermit.

9 *HERMIT*—The Higher Self that will guide the person spiritually in the world.

10 *WHEEL OF FORTUNE*—A choice at this point whether to stay with material and worldly matters, or to seek for attainment.

11 *STRENGTH*—One has learnt to live in the world with confidence and with balance. Also one has learned to adapt where necessary.

12 *HANGED MAN*—The initiate; one has taken the first step to enlightenment and, therefore, can view the world with calm surety.

13 *DEATH*—The death of ignorance. The birth of knowledge, as one prepares to become an initiate.

14 *TEMPERANCE*—One has learned to live in the world with harmony and peace.

15 *DEVIL*—The physical ties, the earthly love that must be accommodated with psychic growth. The final realization, that the "real world" is not all.

16 *TOWER*—Disruption of one's complacence. The first doubts of only being a physical person in a physical world.

17 *STAR*—The quiet that comes from knowing someone can share and assist with life's passage.

18 *MOON*—First awareness that there is more than the physical self. Vacillating and uncertainty of whether to act or not.

19 *SUN*—Worldly happiness and contentment with everyday life. This has to be achieved before spiritual growth can ever take place.

20 *JUDGEMENT*—The family unit. A happy personal life.

21 *WORLD*—The starting point. The material plane. All chances are, however, contained within this sphere, material and spiritual.

This interpretation of the Trumps can, in some ways, be applied to divination, however on their deeper levels these symbols touch upon the very reason for the existence of tarot cards: they represent a pictorial view of a person's spiritual development for those who choose that path.

WEST COUNTRY "TELL" STORIES

These were not called Rune stones but "Tell" stones, and were simply a method of divination.

"Tell" stones were made from clay and were rounded into fairly thick stone shapes. Some were made into a definite ball shape and these were rolled within a wooden frame, about two feet square.

The flatter ones were preferable, though, as they could be thrown on a table or on a flat surface without rolling away.

One stone, which represented the querant, was fashioned of plain clay. It was placed on the table, with the other stones held in two cupped hands as the question was asked. These were then thrown onto the table towards the querant stone. The stones landing nearest the querant stone were closer in time, or importance.

Any groups of stones were read in conjunction with each other. Those that landed with the symbol hidden were removed,

as they were not communicating. If one landed on its side then its answer was "iffy" and could go either way.

Although this was a very simple method, with practice a lot could be obtained from these stones. As with any method of divination, the more they were used the more the practitioner learned of their meanings.

The tell stones had the following symbols on them:

A *five barred gate* — News, letters, ideas.

Some water — Journeys, distance to be crossed symbolically, someone travelling.

An *even-armed cross* — Parting, angry words, quarrels, bad feeling.

A *door* — A death of something, a finishing, some kind of severing.

A *ring* — Marriage or a joining of some kind, either people or things.

A *gold spot* — Health, wealth, happiness.

A *crescent moon* — A waiting time, possibly a woman involved; can mean "use your intuition."

A *silver spot* — Hopes, wishes, dreams and ambitions.

An *apple* — The fruition of something; a harvest; combined with the gold spot, could mean the birth of something new.

These, with the plain stone to represent the querant, are the complete set of "Tell" stones. They can be made from handicraft clay, a stone colour being used and the emblems painted in colours, or coloured clay can be used, a different colour for each, and the symbols painted on in a complementary colour. I do not think it matters if the colours are altered, as long as the user knows which is which.

They need to be about an inch in diameter, as any larger size is difficult to hold. The querant stone can be of any size, but was usually uniform with the others. The querant stone was invariably green.

RITE OF PAN

The glade in the wood is alive with the scent
Of mosses and bracken and briar;
But through it all like a thread of mystic silk
Is the scent from the cauldron fire.
Candles glow round the Circle's edge,
On censer and cords and knife;
As thirteen meet hand in hand,
In celebration of all life.
They dance their dance in mystic moves,
As only they know how,
And through them all runs
The power that proves,
That right in the here and now;
The Old Way is the right Way,
Has been since the dawn of man,
And so beneath the Moon's soft ray,
They rejoice in the Great God Pan.

Rhiannon

EPILOGUE

From a Witch woman, whose
Witch man has gone on before...

When it is time to love again,
And you reach out to take my hand;
With perfect love and trust we'll go,
Together, to our secret land;
And you will take the cup my sweet,
And drink it down, and down again;
But ever full of lover's wine,
For you my dear it will remain.
For you and I are halves of one
Eternal soul, that ever stays
True to itself; though earthly form,
Many times itself betrays.
But the golden cup stays ever full,
That you may drink and be refreshed,
Though Fate and Chance may sunder us—
For a while, yet ever blest;
Are we to know, that in the end,
We are each others lover-friend

Rhiannon

Index